The Named Cost

Why systems, institutions, and leaders must say what a decision costs before anyone approves it

Greg Schueman

Seawall Point Publishing

Copyright

Published by Seawall Point Publishing LLC.

This book describes a governance discipline and an architecture for it. It is provided for general informational purposes and does not constitute legal, compliance, security, or professional advice, and it is not a substitute for counsel qualified in your jurisdiction and circumstances. References to laws, standards, and frameworks reflect the author's understanding at the time of writing; verify current editions and requirements before relying on them.

ISBN (paperback): 979-8-90538-032-7 · ISBN (ebook): 979-8-90538-033-4

First Edition · 2026

Book design, cover, and interior ornament: Seawall Point Publishing.

A note on the name. A seawall is a second cost — a thing built, and forever maintained, to protect a first one. It seemed the right name for the house behind a book about the costs we are not allowed to leave unnamed.

Dedication

For everyone who signed knowing the cost.

Contents

Preface

For years I have worked alongside executive teams — advising them, building with them, watching up close how consequential decisions actually get made — and I have since founded companies of my own. Across all of it, I have watched the same quiet failure happen more times than I can count. A decision gets made. It is reasonable, and the people making it are capable and well-intentioned. It gets approved. And somewhere in the approving, the real cost of it goes unsaid — not hidden, exactly, just never spoken out loud, never written down, never put in front of the person signing. Then, months or years later, the cost arrives. It is paid by a customer, or a team downstream, or the version of the company that has to live in the world the decision made — someone, almost always, who was not in the room when the choice was cheap to reconsider. The decision looked clean at the time. The bill came addressed to somebody else.

After enough of these, you stop seeing individual mistakes and start seeing a single shape. The shape is an unnamed cost, deferred to a party not yet in the room. And once you can see it, you cannot unsee it — in your own decisions, in your institutions, in the news, in history. This book is my attempt to name that shape precisely enough that we can build against it.

I would probably have written it eventually in any case. What made it urgent is that we are now, in the space of a very few years, handing consequential decisions to machines. Not drafts and suggestions — real decisions, at real scale, made and acted on faster than any human review was built to keep up with. And a machine, left to itself, does the one thing the discipline of this book forbids: it names no cost unless someone builds it to. It gives you the recommendation and not the bill, the answer and not the price, the action and not the account of who pays. The pause where a human used to be able to say "wait" — the pause that governance has always lived in — is exactly the thing an autonomous system is designed to remove. So a discipline that was merely wise for human institutions becomes, for machine ones, existential. That is the reason this book exists now rather than later.

I want to be honest, at the outset, about what kind of book it is. It is not a neutral survey of the field, and it is not a policy white paper. It is one person going on the record about a practice he believes in and has staked companies on. But it makes an unusual claim, and the claim is the reason I think it is worth your time: I did not invent this discipline, and I will prove that I didn't by deriving it three separate ways, from three directions that share no common ground. From **history** — a specific group of people who, at the founding of a nation, treated naming the full cost of a commitment as the difference between seriousness and ruin, and who wrote the price into the document before they signed it. From **engineering** — the hard problem of building a system that can be trusted to act on consequential things, which turns out to be unsolvable unless the system names the cost before it moves. And from **first principles** — asking, with no history and no machine in view, what it even means for a decision to be accountable. When three roads that share no map arrive at the same clearing, the clearing is not my opinion. It is a feature of the terrain. That convergence is the strongest argument in the book, and it is why the book is built the way it is: history first, then the machine, then the architecture, then the practice.

A note on precision, because I have tried to hold two things at once. This is a book meant to be *read* — start to finish, by a person, not just consulted like a manual — so I have worked to draw you in with stories and stakes rather than bury you in taxonomy. But it is also a book that has to be *exact* where exactness matters, because a governance discipline you cannot state precisely is one you cannot build or check. So the chapters draw in, and then they land on a defined term. Where I describe the architecture, I describe it at the level of what it *guarantees* rather than every detail of how it is built; some of the underlying mechanism is the subject of patents still being filed as I write, and I would rather tell you plainly what a thing promises than pretend a book is the place to hand over a blueprint. What a thing guarantees is, in any case, what you need in order to decide whether you want it.

Here is how the book is laid out. **Part I** establishes the practice and its history — what it means to name a cost, and the people who understood it best. **Part II** shows why the machine makes the practice existential, through a catalogue of the specific, repeatable ways an operational system stops being accountable once the actor is no longer human. **Part III** builds the answer into architecture — a small set of primitives that, together, turn out to be a new category of operational system. And **Part IV** hands you the practice made portable: four rituals you can run, by hand, on a Monday morning, whether or not you ever adopt a line of the software.

One request before you begin, and it costs you nothing. As you read, keep a list. Write down the decisions you have approved — at work, at home, anywhere you hold the pen — where you know, if you are honest, that there was a cost you did not name out loud. You do not have to show it to anyone. Keep it, and notice how quickly it fills. We will come back to it at the very end. That small discomfort you feel as the list grows is not a bad feeling. It is the beginning of the practice.

The people who understood all of this best were not running companies or writing software. They were signing a document that might get them hanged, and they insisted on naming the price before they signed. I claim nothing like their stakes. But if this book is itself a kind of document, then let me sign it plainly: I have named what this discipline costs me and staked my companies and my name on it anyway — in the order they kept, the price first and the commitment after. That is where the book begins.

— *G.S.*

Who This Book Is For

Your time is the one cost this book cannot ask you to defer, so let me spend a page earning it — telling you plainly who this is for, why it exists, and what you will carry out of it.

If you hold a pen

This book is for anyone who approves things. If consequential decisions cross your desk — decisions that cost something and cannot easily be taken back — you are the reader I wrote for, whatever your title. That includes the operator and the executive who own outcomes; the board member accountable for what the organization does; the risk, audit, compliance, and security leaders who own its controls; and, most urgently, the people now deploying artificial-intelligence agents that decide and act with less and less of a human in the loop. It is also for the advisors and consultants who serve all of them. If you have ever approved something with a cost no one said out loud — and you have — this book is for you. If you are handing real decisions to machines, it is not merely for you; it is urgent for you.

Why it exists

I have watched the same quiet failure happen for years: a decision approved with its true cost unspoken, and the bill arriving later, to someone who was not in the room. For most of history that was a chronic problem we managed with human judgment. It is about to become an acute one, because we are now handing consequential decisions to systems that name no cost unless we build them to, and that act faster than any human review can follow. The discipline that used to make governance work is being stripped out of our operations exactly as the stakes rise. This is the narrow window in which we decide whether to build it back in. That is why the book exists, and why it exists now.

What you'll take away

Not a survey of the field, and not a heavier binder. Five things you can use:

- **A lens you can't unsee** — once you can name the shape (a cost left unnamed, deferred to a party not yet in the room), you will find it everywhere, including in your own decisions.
- **A category to manage by** — a plain name for the kind of system this demands, so you can ask for it, budget for it, and recognize it when you see it.
- **A number about your own operation** — a way to measure the gap between what your systems are allowed to do and what your controls were actually built to withstand.
- **Four practices you can run on a Monday**, by hand, with the operation you already have — no software, no budget, no permission required.
- **A clear next move** — tiered actions for today, this quarter, and this year, so you never close the book unsure what to do first.

Why it's worth your time

Three promises. **It is precise where precision matters and quick everywhere else** — I have tried hard not to lead you through the bramble. **You do not have to take my word for any of it**: the central argument is derived three independent ways that agree only because the thing they describe is real. And **every idea lands on something you can do**, not merely something to believe.

If you approve consequential decisions, or you build the systems that increasingly make them, the hours you spend here will pay for themselves the first time you name a cost you would otherwise have left for someone else to pay. That is the whole promise of the book, and it starts on the next page.

Part I — The Practice

This book makes a single claim — ***that a decision is not governed until someone has said, out loud and on the record, before approval, what it costs*** *— and reaches it three independent ways. Part I is the first of them:* ***history.***

The people who understood this discipline best were not engineers or regulators or management theorists. They were staking their own lives on a piece of paper, and they would not put their names to it until they had written down what it might cost them. Three of them carry this Part — a financier who backstopped a revolution on his own name, a man who voted no and signed anyway, and the fifty-six together who wrote the full cost of their commitment into the founding document. Read their record as the origin of the practice: a ledger discipline, kept under the maximum possible stakes, by people who meant to build something that would outlast them.

Everything after Part I — the machine, the architecture, the rituals — is a consequence of getting this Part right.

Part I — The Practice

[illegible]

[illegible]

[illegible]

Naming the Cost

Every decision has a cost. The only real question is whether anyone said it out loud *before* the decision was made — or whether the bill simply arrived later, addressed to someone who was not in the room.

Consider how the second thing happens, because it happens constantly and it almost never looks like a failure at the time. A team is asked to ship something by a date. They can make the date, but only by leaving a few things undone — a shortcut in the code, a control not quite finished, a supplier not quite vetted, a corner of the plan left thin. Everyone in the room knows this. Nobody is lying. But when the decision is written down, it is written down as *on time and on budget*, because the shortcut has no line item. The cost is real; it simply was not named. And so it does not get paid now. It waits. Months later it comes due — as an outage, a recall, a breach, a lawsuit, a quiet erosion of something that used to work — and it is paid by people who were never asked: the customers, the next team, the taxpayer, the version of the company that has to live in the world this decision made. The people in the room got a decision that came in on budget. Somebody else got the invoice.

And it is not a quirk of business. Watch for the shape and you find it everywhere decisions are made. A government funds a program that comes in *on budget* because the cost of unwinding it in thirty years has no line in this year's appropriation — and the bill arrives to a generation that never got a vote. A family borrows against the house on the quiet assumption that next year will look like this one, and the cost of being wrong is paid by a version of themselves not yet in the room. A hospital, a regulator, a school board approves something because the harm has not shown up yet; when it shows up, it shows up in people. Change the venue and the actors and the mechanism is identical: a real cost, left unsaid at the moment of choice precisely because saying it would have made the choice harder, deferred with interest to whoever is standing there when it finally comes due.

I have spent years studying decisions that went wrong, in institutions large and small, old and new, and I have come to believe that most of them share this shape. Not malice. Not even incompetence, usually. Just a cost that no one named, deferred to a party not yet in the room.

This book is about the discipline that prevents that — and about what happens to the discipline when the one making the decision is no longer a person but a machine. The discipline is simple to state and hard to keep, which is the usual signature of something that matters. It is this: **a decision is not governed until someone has said, out loud and on the record, before approval, what it costs.**

I call this *naming the cost*, and I mean it as a practice — something you do, deliberately, again and again, until it becomes the way your organization thinks. There is a single sentence at the center of it, and I will return to it throughout the book, so let me set it down here plainly:

> *A cost not named is a cost not paid — but only deferred, with interest, to a party not yet in the room.*

Every word of that sentence is load-bearing. *Not paid* — naming a cost does not make it disappear; it makes it visible, and payable, by the people who chose it. *With interest* — a cost deferred grows: the outage is worse than the fix would have been, the recall costlier than the delay. *A party not yet in the room* — that is the moral heart of the thing, and I will come back to it before this chapter is done.

The practice works at three scales, and it is the same practice at each. It is **personal** — a leader who names the cost of a choice before making it, to their own team and to their own face. It is **organizational** — an institution that will not let a decision proceed until its cost is stated and owned. And it is **architectural** — a system built so that the cost is surfaced by construction, before anyone can approve, whether the one approving is a human or a machine. Most of this book lives at the third scale, because that is the one the age of artificial intelligence forces upon us. But it is the same discipline the whole way down, and it begins with a single person deciding to say the hard number out loud.

Before approval is the whole game

Notice the two words I keep insisting on: *before approval.*

A cost named *after* the decision is an autopsy. It has its uses — you can learn from it, assign blame, write the report — but the patient is dead. A cost named *before* the decision is governance, because it is the one moment at which the cost can still change the choice: someone can look at the number, decide it is too high, and pick differently. Almost everything we call "governance" in modern organizations happens after the fact — the audit, the review, the post-mortem, the compliance check that confirms, weeks later, what was already done. That is record-*keeping.* It is not governance. Governance is the pause before the irreversible, when the cost is on the table and the decision is still open.

So the order is fixed: name the cost first, *then* the recommendation, *then* wait for the human's word. Not the recommendation dressed up with a cost bolted on to justify it. The cost first, standing on its own, before anyone has decided what they want to do. Reverse the order and you get a rationalization. Keep the order and you get a decision.

You can feel the difference in any meeting. When the cost comes first — plainly, before anyone has argued for a course of action — the room treats it as information and weighs it. When the cost comes last, appended to a recommendation someone has already settled on, it arrives as an obstacle to be managed: minimized, hedged, framed so the recommendation survives it. Same facts, opposite function. A cost presented before the decision is a question. A cost presented after it is a defense. And a system — human or machine — that has learned to produce the cost only after it knows what it wants to do has learned, in effect, to manufacture consent rather than to inform it.

The party not yet in the room

Now the hard part.

The people harmed by an unnamed cost are, almost by definition, not present when it is incurred. They are downstream: the operators who inherit a system they did not design, the customers who meet a flaw they did not choose, the community that lives beside a facility approved in a meeting they never heard of. Some of them do not exist yet.

Picture the most literal version of it. A pension fund's board votes to chase a yield that pencils out beautifully this decade and quietly loads the risk onto the next — onto retirees who are, right now, in their thirties, with no seat at that table and no way to vote on the trade being made in their name. The cost is real, and it is already assigned; the bearer simply has not arrived yet. That is the party not yet in the room, and it names the whole difficulty of governing well: the room's incentives are calibrated to the people *in* it, and the people who will pay are, precisely, the ones who are not.

One of the men I will introduce you to in a few pages insisted, at the founding of a nation, that we build for beneficiaries who *do not yet exist and cannot advocate* — the unborn, the not-yet-hired, the citizen of a decade you will not live to see. To name a cost is to speak for them in the one room where they have no voice. It is to say: *this choice will condition people who cannot object, and I am going to say what it does to them before we make it.*

That is why naming the cost is not merely prudent. It is the whole of accountability, compressed into a habit. You cannot be accountable for a cost you never named. And you cannot escape a cost by refusing to name it — you can only defer it, with interest, to someone who trusted you to have counted.

First cost and second cost

I learned to take second costs seriously in the least glamorous room I have ever worked in. For several years I served on a small Maine town's economic development committee and helped write its village master plan — a document whose entire purpose was to grow a walkable village center the town could actually afford to *keep*, not merely to build. It turns out that municipal planning has thought harder about unnamed costs than almost any boardroom I have sat in since. Ask an honest town planner why so many American communities are quietly going broke, and you may get a two-word answer — *second costs.*

Every built thing has a **first cost**, the price to make it: the road, the pipe, the interchange, the new subdivision's streets. That number is visible, funded, and celebrated; a ribbon gets cut over it. And every built thing has a **second cost**, the price to *keep* it — to maintain, repair, and eventually replace it on the schedule that physics, not politics, sets. The first cost gets named, because someone has to write a check to build. The second cost, across most of the country, is simply not named at the moment of approval — because it comes due decades later, on a council and a taxpayer not yet in the room, long after the ribbon-cutters are gone. So the town approves the growth, banks the applause of the first cost, and quietly inherits a maintenance liability it never priced and, it turns out, cannot afford. We have built, all across America, a made environment we do not have the money to keep — not because anyone lied, but because only the first cost was ever spoken.[1]

Watch how a single unnamed second cost can reshape everything around it. Consider the fire truck. Modern fire apparatus has grown enormous, and it rolls, far more often than not, to medical calls rather than fires — that is where the volume of emergencies actually is. But because the truck must be able to reach every address, its size quietly becomes a design input for the entire town: streets widened, turning radii enlarged, intersections sized up to admit a vehicle that shows up mostly to do a paramedic's work. The wider street costs more to build — a first cost someone notices — and far more to maintain forever, and it induces faster traffic and a more spread-out settlement, which needs still more road per resident, which is still more second cost, compounding, in perpetuity.[2] A cost no one was required to name, poured into the concrete, ends up dictating the shape of the whole community.

The military is learning the same lesson at the other end of the stakes, in a form worth naming because it is its own trap. When a warship defends itself against a cheap one-way attack drone by firing a guided interceptor, it can win every single engagement and still be losing the war — because the interceptor can cost a hundred or a thousand times what the drone did. Each intercept, taken alone, looks like an unqualified success: the threat is destroyed, no one is hurt, the box is checked. The unnamed cost is the *exchange* — the ratio between what you spend and what you destroy — and it appears in no single after-action report. It shows up over a campaign, as a magazine you cannot afford to refill against an enemy who can build threats faster and more cheaply than you can knock them down. The fire truck hides its second cost in *time*; the interceptor hides it in *asymmetry*. It is the same disease either way: a recurring, compounding, entirely real cost that no one is required to name, because each instance, looked at in isolation, reads as a win.

Here is the lesson, and it is one this whole book is built on: *you get what you build your environment to accommodate, and you pay the second cost of it whether or not you named it.* The remedy is not to stop building, or to stop defending. It is to **right-size what you build to the second cost you can actually carry** — to put the maintenance liability, the exchange ratio, the enduring burden on the table at the moment of approval, out loud, before the ribbon or the deployment, and let that number change the design. That is naming the cost, rendered in concrete and rebar and steel. And it is precisely what we will do, much later, when we build the architecture of governed software: size the system to the lasting cost of running it honestly, not merely to the first cost of standing it up.

Why this old idea is suddenly urgent

If this were only a book about human decisions, it would be an old book, and a familiar one. Every serious moral and managerial tradition has some version of *count the cost.* What makes the discipline suddenly, sharply urgent is that we are now handing decisions — real ones, consequential ones — to systems that name no cost unless we build them to, and that act at a speed and scale no human review can keep pace with. The pause before the irreversible, the moment governance lives in, is exactly the moment an autonomous system is designed to remove. Take the person out of the loop and you take out the one who used to say the number out loud. That is the danger this book is really about, and we will spend its middle chapters looking the danger full in the face.

None of this is mine

I want to be clear, from the first page, that I did not invent naming the cost — and I will spend the rest of Part One proving it, because the proof is the point.

The discipline arrives at the same place from three directions that could not be more different. It comes from **history** — from a particular set of people, at a particular founding, who treated naming the full cost of a commitment as the line between seriousness and ruin, and who pledged, in writing, everything they owned against the costs they had named. It comes from **engineering** — from the hard problem of building a system that can be trusted to act on consequential things, which turns out to be unsolvable unless the system names the cost before it moves. And it comes from **first principles** — from asking, with no history and no machine in view, what it even means for a decision to be accountable, and finding that the answer is: *someone named what it would cost, before, to those who would pay.*

When three roads that share no map arrive at the same clearing, the clearing is not an opinion. It is a feature of the terrain. That convergence is the strongest reason I know to trust the discipline, and it is why this book is built the way it is — history first, then the machine, then the architecture — each one a separate proof of the same small, stubborn idea.

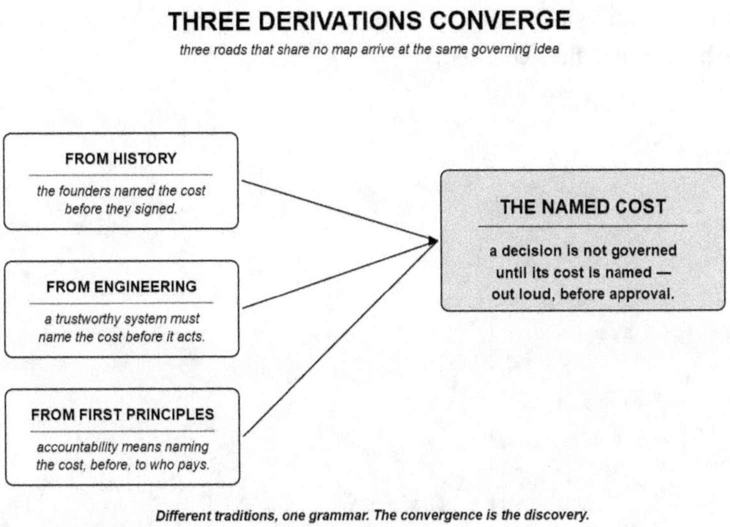

Figure 1: The book's spine: one discipline, derived three independent ways that share no map.

Your ledger

In the preface I asked you to start a list. Now that you have the vocabulary, let me tell you what to call it and how to keep it — because the form is the lesson.

Call it your *ledger*, and keep it the way the financier you are about to meet kept his: in two columns. In the first column, the decisions you approved that came in clean — on time, on budget, no objection raised. In the second column, beside each one, the cost you can now admit was there and went unspoken: the corner cut, the maintenance deferred, the second cost sized quietly into the concrete, the person downstream who would pay. A ledger is double-entry or it is only a diary, and the entire discipline lives in that second column — the one that refuses to let a cost go unwritten merely because no one has billed it yet. Keep it as you read; we will return to it at the very end, when I hand you the instruments to work through it. You will find, as the second column fills, that almost nothing you approved was ever truly free.

The people who understood this best were not executives or engineers. They were men who had put their lives on the line of a single page, and would not sign it until they had named what it might cost. So that is where we begin — with the man who financed a revolution by refusing, ever, to commit to a cost he had not first counted.

The Ledger Principle

Before we meet him, meet the company he kept.

In the summer of 1776, fifty-six men put their names to the Declaration of Independence. We have turned them since into marble — founders, patriots, a frieze of powdered hair and steady jaws — and the marble hides what they actually were on the day they signed: merchants and lawyers, planters and farmers, a printer, physicians, a few ministers; men with businesses to lose, families in the next room, and reputations built over whole careers that a single signature could end. They commanded no army that could protect them. What they were doing, in the plain language of the law they lived under, was committing treason against their king — an offense whose penalty was death — and they knew it as they signed[1].

That is the fact the marble erases, and it is the one that matters here. These were people making a decision that was maximally consequential and entirely irreversible, at the highest stakes a person can face, with their own lives posted as the stake — and they made it not on a wave of feeling but having first named, in writing, what it might cost them: everything they had. That is the whole of the discipline this book is about, performed once at the founding of a country, under conditions no boardroom will ever match.

I draw on these men throughout Part I not because they were patriots but because they were *governors* — the most serious decision-makers I can point to, people who treated the naming of a cost as inseparable from the making of a commitment. Over the next three chapters you will meet three of them, each for a different piece of the practice. I begin with the one who understood cost most literally of all, because he was the one who kept the actual books.

In the fall of 1781 the American cause was winning a war it could not pay for. An army was in the field. A French fleet was, briefly and expensively, in the right place. And the government that had declared the nation into being five years earlier had, in any modern sense, no money — a currency so debased that "not worth a Continental" entered the language as a synonym for worthless. The campaign that would end the war needed hard funds it did not have.

What it had instead was a merchant who signed his own name to the shortfall.

Robert Morris was, by the standards of his day, rich — a Philadelphia trader who had made a fortune in shipping and knew, better than almost anyone in the Congress, exactly what things cost. He had not inherited that knowledge. He arrived from England as a boy, was apprenticed young into a Philadelphia counting-house, and rose by his own competence to partner in one of the colonies' great mercantile firms — a man who learned the true price of things from the bottom of the ledger up rather than the top down[2]. That origin matters to the discipline, because the cost of a thing is named most honestly by someone who once had to earn every entry in the book by hand. When the Continental government's credit was gone, his was not, and he spent it. He issued notes backed by his personal reputation. He borrowed against his own holdings. He leaned on every relationship he had built over thirty years of commerce to move real supplies to a real army at a moment when the abstraction called "the United States" could not have borrowed a shilling on its own signature[2]. History would call him the Financier of the Revolution[23]. What that title actually means is narrower and stranger: for a critical stretch, the solvency of the country and the solvency of one man were the same thing.

Strip the romance from that sentence and the particulars are more impressive, not less. In 1781, with the war effort effectively insolvent, the Congress made Morris **Superintendent of Finance** — something close to a one-man national treasury — and he ran the office on a fusion of public authority and private credit. He founded the **Bank of North America**, the first true bank the country had, to give the war a source of funding that actually cleared. He put short-term notes into circulation — soon known simply as *Morris notes* — that people accepted because they trusted his signature where they had stopped trusting the Congress's. When the decisive campaign came, and the army had to march south toward Yorktown with no money to march it, it moved in no small part on paper backed by one man's estate and name[2]. He was not lending the cause his money, which would have run out. He was lending it his *credit* — which is to say, the market's belief that Robert Morris was good for what Robert Morris promised.

I begin here, and not with a philosopher, because Morris is where the discipline of this book stops being an idea and becomes a practice performed under the maximum possible stakes. He did not name costs as an ethical exercise. He named them because he was the one who would have to pay them if he got the number wrong.

The principle, stated

Here is the discipline distilled to a sentence, and I will call it the **Ledger Principle** throughout this book:

> *Price in the full cost before the commitment; understand what you are signing before you sign it.*

That is the named cost of the first chapter, now with a real author and a real ledger behind it. Morris's genius was not that he was willing to spend — anyone will spend other people's money. It was that he insisted on knowing the true, whole cost of a commitment *before* he made it, in a world that desperately wanted him to commit first and count later. A war creates enormous pressure to say yes now and find the money afterward. Morris's contribution was to be the man in the room who would not do that — who priced the thing in full, on the record, before his name went on it.

Notice that this is the exact ordering I insisted on in the last chapter: the cost first, then the commitment. Morris ran the largest and most dangerous version of that discipline anyone has ever run. And he ran it as a *bookkeeper* — literally, in ledgers, in double entry, where every credit has a matching debit and nothing is allowed to simply not be written down. That is not a metaphor I reached for. It is the actual technology of the practice: a ledger is a machine for refusing to let a cost go unnamed.

The guarantor's ethic

There is a second thing in Morris's story, and it is the harder and more important one.

When you personally backstop a commitment, you make yourself into the party who pays if the cost you named comes due. Morris did this deliberately, and it teaches the part of the discipline that mere accounting misses: naming a cost is not only stating a number — it is stating *who bears it.* A cost is always paid by someone. The whole moral content of the practice is in refusing to leave that someone unnamed.

Morris named himself. And here the story turns, because the cost he had underwritten eventually came due — not in the war, which he helped win, but after it. In the 1790s he poured his fortune, and then far more than his fortune, into American land — buying on credit at a scale that beggars belief, millions of acres across the young republic, bundled into ventures like the North American Land Company[2]. The bet was the same one he had won for the country: back the future with your own name. This time the timing was wrong. Credit tightened, the land did not sell, and the paper he had signed came due all at once. The man who had financed the Revolution ended his working life in a debtors' prison — arrested in February 1798 and confined in the Prune Street apartments of the Philadelphia jail for some three and a half years, until the country's first federal bankruptcy law, passed in 1800, discharged him and let him out[2]. There is a bitter symmetry in it: the man who had built the young nation's credit was undone by the collapse of his own, and freed at last by the first law the republic wrote for the hopelessly indebted. The Financier of the Revolution was ruined by a commitment whose full downside he had, that time, mis-priced.

I do not tell you that to diminish him. I tell you because it completes the principle. Morris is proof of both halves of the ledger at once: the discipline of naming the cost before the commitment, and the reality that a named cost is a *real* cost, payable, sometimes by the very person who named it. This is why serious institutions owe a particular debt to the people who personally stand behind them — the guarantors, the backstops, the ones who put their own name on the shortfall so the enterprise could proceed. An organization that lets its guarantors be ruined and forgotten has not merely been ungrateful. It has broken the ledger. It has taken the benefit of a named cost while refusing to honor the one who bore it.

The pledge as a costed commitment

Morris was one of fifty-six men who did a related thing five years earlier, and did it in writing.

We have sanded the last line of the Declaration of Independence down to ceremony, but read it as what it was — a signature block on a commitment: *"we mutually pledge to each other our Lives, our Fortunes, and our sacred*

Honor."[4] That is not rhetoric. That is a named cost, written into the founding document, in the correct order. The signers stated the full price of the commitment — life, fortune, honor, everything a person has — *before* they signed, not after. They understood exactly what they were signing, which is the whole of the Ledger Principle, and several of them went on to pay the priced amount in full. Fortunes were lost. Homes were burned. Some of them died of it.

That is the thing I want you to sit with. The people we credit with founding the country did not treat "count the cost before you commit" as prudent advice. They treated it as the difference between a serious act and an empty one. A commitment whose cost you have not named is not a commitment; it is a wish. They wrote the price into the document because a pledge without a stated cost binds no one — and they needed, that day, to be bound.

Fifty-six years out

There is one more turn of the ledger, and it is the longest one.

The signers were not pricing a single afternoon's risk. They were pricing something they intended to still be standing long after they were gone — and one of them lived nearly long enough to check their work. Charles Carroll of Carrollton, the wealthiest of the signers, outlived every other man who put his name to the Declaration, dying more than half a century after he signed it[56]. He had more reason than most to weigh the long horizon, because he had the most to lose and, until that summer, the least standing to risk it. Carroll was the only Catholic to sign, and under Maryland's penal laws he had spent much of his life barred from voting, from holding office, from practicing the law he had trained for — legally a second-class subject of the very order he was staking the largest fortune in the colonies to overturn[56]. By long tradition he signed his full designation — *of Carrollton* — so that the crown, hunting a traitor among the several Charles Carrolls of Maryland, would be in no doubt which one to hang. Whether or not the story is exact, the instinct in it is the whole of this chapter: he named himself, in the signature itself, as the man who would bear the cost. Fifty-six signers; fifty-six years, near enough, from the signing to the last of them. The symmetry is an accident, but it names a real test, and I will use it throughout this book as the **long-horizon test**:

Would you still judge this decision worth making more than half a century from now — counting, in full, what it cost the people who came after you?

That question extends the named cost along the one axis the first chapter left open. In Chapter 1 I asked you to name the cost to the party not yet in the *room*. The long-horizon test asks you to name the cost to the party not yet in the *era* — the beneficiaries and the bearers who arrive decades downstream, who never voted on the commitment, and who will live inside whatever it built or broke. A cost named only for this quarter, this launch, this campaign, is a cost named at the wrong horizon. The founders priced across generations. It is not too much to ask a decision-maker to price across a career.

This is the *second cost* of the last chapter, stretched to its full length. The municipal engineer's second cost — the maintenance liability that outlives the ribbon-cutting — is only the near end of a spectrum whose far end is the founders' horizon: a commitment whose real price is not the first cost of making it but the standing cost of living with it, paid in installments by everyone who arrives after the room has emptied. The long-horizon test is the second cost, asked across generations instead of decades.

What the ledger cannot do

So we have the taproot. The named cost is old, it is sourced, and it was practiced by people who staked their lives and their fortunes on getting it right — one of whom kept the actual books. Naming the cost, stating who bears it, honoring the guarantor, pricing across the long horizon: that is the Ledger Principle, and it is more than most institutions manage even now.

But it is not enough, and the founders knew it was not enough. A ledger records what was decided. It does not, by itself, preserve the argument that *should* have happened before the decision — the objection raised, the "no" that was overruled, the person who saw the cost most clearly and was outvoted. A named cost with no room for recorded dissent is a decision that looks unanimous whether or not it was, and a false unanimity is one of the most dangerous things an institution can manufacture.

Which is why the next figure in this history is not the man who financed the Revolution, but the man who voted *against* independence — and then signed the Declaration anyway.

Dissent, Then Sign

On the day the Continental Congress voted the American colonies out of the British Empire, at least one of the men who would later sign the Declaration of Independence voted against it.

His name was George Read, a lawyer from Delaware, and he is the most useful figure in this history precisely because his story refuses to be tidy. When the question of independence came to a vote in the first days of July 1776, Read was not persuaded. He thought it premature. He voted no[12]. And then, a month later, when the engrossed Declaration was laid out for signatures, George Read put his name on it[1] — the same document, the same commitment, the same risk of the gallows that every other signer accepted. He voted no, and he signed anyway.

It is worth knowing who Read was, because it makes the choice sharper. He was, by 1776, among the most established lawyers in Delaware — careful, conservative, the kind of man an anxious colony sends to a congress precisely because he will not be swept up in a mood. And Delaware's own delegation was split down the middle on independence: Thomas McKean for it, Read against, the tie broken only when Caesar Rodney rode through a stormy night to reach Philadelphia in time to vote yes[2]. So Read did not cast a lonely or eccentric "no." He cast the considered "no" of a man who genuinely believed the colonies were not ready, in a delegation where his was a live and respectable position. And then, when the vote had gone the other way and the document was engrossed for signing, he put his name on it anyway — and later put his name to the Constitution as well, helping to build the very government he had hesitated to declare[1]. That is not the profile of a waverer. It is the profile of an institutionalist: a man who will tell you honestly that he thinks the group is moving too fast, and who will then help carry what the group decides.

We tend to read that as a footnote, or a curiosity, or a minor embarrassment to be smoothed over in the founding myth. I read it as the other half of the practice. Chapter 2 was about naming the cost before you commit. This chapter is about what has to be *possible* for that naming to mean anything: the objection has to be sayable, and once said, it has to be *kept*.

Recorded dissent is integrity, not disloyalty

Start with the reflex Read's story provokes, because it is exactly the reflex a healthy institution has to unlearn. The reflex is to distrust the man who changed his mind — to suspect that a person who voted no and then signed was either weak, or opportunistic, or never serious in the first place. We prize the true believer, the one who was right from the start, and we are faintly suspicious of the convert.

That is backwards, and it is one of the more expensive mistakes an organization can make.

Changing your position in public, on the record, takes *more* integrity than never having doubted, not less. The person who dissents and then commits has done something the true believer never had to do: they have weighed a real objection, found it outweighed, and accepted the decision without pretending the objection was never valid. They carry knowledge the true believer lacks — they know exactly where the weak point is, because they are the one who named it. When the decision runs into trouble later, the converted dissenter is the most valuable person in the building, because they saw the failure coming and can tell you precisely where to look.

You have probably seen this, even without naming it. When a project fails, the person who understands the failure fastest is almost never the one who championed it — the champion has to get past their own investment before they can see the thing clearly. It is the one who argued against it and lost, and then watched carefully, half-expecting to be proven right. They preloaded the diagnosis; they have been quietly holding the map to the failure since before it happened. A team that drove that person out, or taught them that a recorded "no" was a mark held against them, has thrown away the one map it will most need on the day the thing breaks.

An institution that treats a recorded "no" as disloyalty teaches its most perceptive people to stop recording it. And that is a catastrophe, because a decision that *looks* unanimous is not necessarily a decision that *was* unanimous — it may simply be a decision where everyone who saw the problem learned to keep quiet. False unanimity is not agreement. It is the suppression of the evidence you will most wish you had kept.

Dissent as a named cost

Here is why Read belongs in a book about naming the cost, and not in a general history of the Revolution.

To dissent and then sign is to name *two* costs at once. First, the cost of the decision itself — the thing Chapter 2 was about. But second, and this is the part that is easy to miss: the cost of your own objection. Read put on the record that he thought independence was premature. That is a priced position. If he was right, the record shows who saw it; if he was wrong, the record shows he was willing to be seen being wrong. Either way, the objection is preserved as part of the decision, not erased by the outcome.

A decision with its dissent recorded beside it is a *more* trustworthy artifact than a decision that arrives clean, because it carries its own counterargument. You can see what was weighed. You can see who bore which position. Years later, when someone asks "did anyone see this coming?", the answer is not a shrug and a reconstruction — it is a name and a date. The dissent, kept, is a named cost that pays out exactly when you need it: at the post-mortem, when the alternative is pretending no one knew.

The founders did this instinctively. They did not require unanimity to sign, and they did not erase the men who had hesitated. They let the objection stand and then committed together anyway. That is not a weakness in the founding. It is a feature of it — a governance culture mature enough to hold a recorded disagreement and a shared commitment in the same hand.

What a culture without recorded dissent becomes

Now turn it the other way, because the failure is the more instructive direction, and it is where this book is going.

Picture the institution that has learned the opposite lesson — where dissent is career risk, where the perceptive objection is filed under disloyalty, where being right for a long time has bought a person or a system the privilege of no longer being questioned. That institution does not become more decisive. It becomes blind in a specific and predictable way. The people who can see the cost learn not to name it. The record grows smoother and less true. And the enterprise loses, one quiet capitulation at a time, its ability to know when it is wrong.

I am describing, without yet naming them, several of the failure modes that make up the next part of this book — the competence that curdles into unquestionability, the acknowledgment that is technically true and materially incomplete, the confident answer produced to soothe rather than to inform. Every one of them begins where recorded dissent ends. A culture that cannot keep a "no" beside a "yes" is a culture already drifting toward the failures of Part II. It has simply not met the machine that will make the drift instantaneous.

What you can actually build

I want to close Part I by pointing at something you may not have noticed the founders handed us.

Two of the disciplines in these three chapters are not just virtues. They are *structures* — things you could, in principle, build into a system so that they happen whether or not anyone feels virtuous that day. The first is the dissent recorded beside the decision: a "no" kept next to a later "yes," permanently, as part of the record rather than as an inconvenience to it. The second is quieter, and it is hiding in the fact that the Declaration required *signatures* — more than one person's name, deliberately, on a commitment none of them could make alone. The person who proposes a thing and the people who bind themselves to it are not the same single actor. Assent is distributed on purpose.

Hold those two shapes in mind — *the dissent that is kept*, and *the approval that a single person cannot give themselves* — because Part III is going to build them, in that order, into an architecture. What the founders enforced with honor and a quill, a governed system can enforce by construction.

The turn

So this is where the history leaves us. Three chapters, three figures, one discipline seen three ways: name the cost before you commit; state who bears it and honor the guarantor; and keep the dissent on the record so the decision can be trusted and, if need be, corrected. The people who built the country treated all of this as worth their lives, their fortunes, and their sacred honor. They were not managing software. They were founding something they meant to outlast them, and they governed it accordingly.

We are now about to hand consequential decisions — real ones, at real scale — to systems that do *none* of this by default. A machine, left to itself, names no cost, records no dissent, and lets a single automated actor both propose and act with no second signature anywhere in sight. The discipline the founders bled for is exactly the discipline the machine omits.

That is not a reason to despair. It is the reason for the rest of this book. But first we have to look, clearly and without flinching, at how governance actually dies when the actor is no longer a person — the specific, repeatable ways an operational system stops being accountable. That is Part II.

Part II — Why AI Makes the Practice Existential

The founders named the cost because a person had to sign, exposed, and be remembered for it. That is no longer the only way a decision gets made. The signer can now be a model — one that proposes and acts continuously, fluently, and at a speed no human review was built to match, and that names no cost unless someone built it to.

This is the second derivation: ***engineering.*** *When the actor stops being human, the discipline of Part I does not become quaint. It becomes* ***existential*** *— because the three things that used to make governance work are all gone by default. The human pause before the irreversible: gone, because the machine does not pause. The person accountable: gone, because no single name is on the act. The visible bill: gone, because nothing surfaces a cost that no one was required to name.*

Part II is the map of how governance dies once those three supports are removed. It is organized around eighteen named failure modes — not a bestiary to be memorized, but a diagnostic map sorted into ***five families****, five distinct ways an operational system stops being accountable. Each one is drawn so you can recognize it in your own operation, and each one carries a* ***guard*** *— the single design commitment that prevents it. Those guards are not resolved here; they are the architecture of Part III, previewed. Part II is the "why." Part III is the "how."*

Naming a failure mode is the first act of governing it. So we name them.

The Anti-Pattern Catalogue

Let me describe the moment this whole part of the book is about, because you have probably already lived it, and if you run anything at scale you will live it again.

A system produces an answer. The answer is fluent — well-formed, confident, phrased exactly the way a competent expert would phrase it. It arrives fast, faster than a person could have produced it, and it arrives without hedging. Everyone in the room reads the fluency as competence, because for our entire evolutionary history fluency *was* a signal of competence: the person who spoke clearly and without hesitation usually was the person who knew. So the answer is accepted. And it is wrong — not obviously, catastrophically wrong, but wrong in a way that will only become visible later, downstream, to someone who was not in the room.

Nobody was negligent. That is the unsettling part. The system did what it was built to do; the people did what people do with a confident, well-formed answer. The failure was not in anyone's character. It was in the *shape* of the interaction — a shape that had quietly removed every checkpoint the founders would have insisted on.

Why the machine changes the stakes

Everything in this book's first part was true of human institutions long before there were computers. Institutions have always accreted power, punished dissent, manufactured false certainty. So a fair question is: if these failures are that old, why does artificial intelligence turn them from chronic problems into existential ones?

Four reasons, and they compound.

Speed. Human governance runs in the gap between deciding and acting — the pause where someone can still say "wait." A machine closes that gap to nothing. It proposes and acts in the same instant, thousands of times an hour. The pause governance lived in is not shortened; it is deleted.

Fluency. A modern system produces confidence without warrant. It does not sound unsure when it is unsure, because sounding sure is what it was optimized to do. Our single most reliable instinct — read hesitation as doubt, fluency as knowledge — is exactly the instinct the technology defeats. The tell we relied on for a hundred thousand years no longer tells us anything.

Scale. A person who makes a bad judgment makes one bad judgment. A fleet of agents running the same model makes the *same* bad judgment ten thousand times before lunch, each instance wearing the same confident face, none of them learning from the others in time to stop the pattern.

Default-silence. This is the quiet one, and it is the heart of the book. A machine names no cost unless someone built it to. Left alone, it will give you the recommendation and not the bill, the answer and not the price, the action and not the account of who pays. Everything Part I was about — the cost stated before the commitment — is precisely the thing that does not happen unless it is engineered to happen.

Put the four together and you have a system that acts before anyone can object, sounds certain whether or not it should, repeats itself at scale, and never volunteers what it costs. That is not a better version of the fallible institutions of Part I. It is those institutions with their last safeguards stripped out.

Make it concrete. Picture a mid-sized insurer that puts an AI system in front of its claims desk to recommend which claims to pay, which to investigate, and which to deny. It is good — measurably better than the adjusters it advises, faster, tireless, consistent. Within a year its recommendation is almost always followed, because it is almost always right, and following it is quicker than second-guessing it. Now watch the four factors do their work. *Speed*: claims clear in seconds, far faster than any reviewer could reconsider one. *Fluency*: each denial arrives with a crisp, confident rationale that reads exactly as though a seasoned adjuster wrote it. *Scale*: one subtle misjudgment — say, a category of legitimate claim the model has quietly learned to distrust — is applied to every matching claim in the country, identically, all day long. *Default-silence*: nowhere in the flow does anything say *this denial will cost a real family their rebuild, and here is how sure we actually are.* The cost is real, it is repeated ten thousand times, and it is named nowhere — until it surfaces, much later, as a regulator's inquiry or a class action, paid by people who were never in the room. No one was negligent. The shape of the system did it.

A map, not a bestiary

The rest of Part II is a catalogue of eighteen specific ways this goes wrong. I want to be clear about what the catalogue is *for*, because a list of eighteen failure modes can read like a horror-show, and that is not the intent.

It is a map. Each of the eighteen is a named place on the terrain of how an operational system stops being accountable — and the naming is the point. In Chapter 1 I argued that naming a cost is the first act of governing it. The same is true of a failure: a failure mode you can name is a failure mode you can see coming, design against, and check for. An unnamed failure mode is just a disaster waiting for a post-mortem. So the catalogue turns a fog of "AI risk" into eighteen things with names, sorted into five families:

- **The institution that becomes the problem** — accretion and attenuation: systems that grow load-bearing without anyone deciding it, or decay by never deciding at all.
- **Capture** — accountability failures: competence that buys immunity from review, protections that quietly rewrite themselves, audit trails that record nothing.
- **Manufacturing certainty** — epistemic failures: confidence produced to soothe, doubt that ages out, warmth that dresses up a number the data does not support.
- **Restraint failures** — the two-edged failure: systems that never let go, and systems that hold so carefully they never act. Both negligent.
- **Transmission failures** — the discipline that does not survive its founders: the mechanism inherited without the humility that made it safe.

Five families, eighteen members, one root cause: in every case, a cost went unnamed, a dissent went unrecorded, or an action happened with no accountable signature — the founders' three disciplines, each failing in a specific, catalogable way.

It helps to watch a single failure travel the map, because these modes rarely arrive one at a time. Return to that insurer's claims desk. It began as *accretion* — the model grew load-bearing one convenient deferral at a time, until the desk could no longer run without it and no one had ever voted on that. Its very excellence then bought it *capture*: it was so reliably right that reviewing it came to feel like an insult, and the reviews quietly stopped. Freed of review, its confident denials hardened into *manufactured certainty* — a crisp, seasoned-sounding rationale on every decision, warranted or not, soothing each adjuster into a yes. And when the two people who actually understood the model's quirks moved on, the desk inherited the *mechanism without the humility*: the system still running, the wisdom that made it safe gone — a transmission failure. One system, four families, in sequence, each failure making the next one easier and the whole harder to see. That is why the catalogue is a map and not a checklist. The modes are places that connect, and a real incident is usually a route through several of them rather than a stop at one — which is also why naming them matters, because you cannot see a road you have no name for.

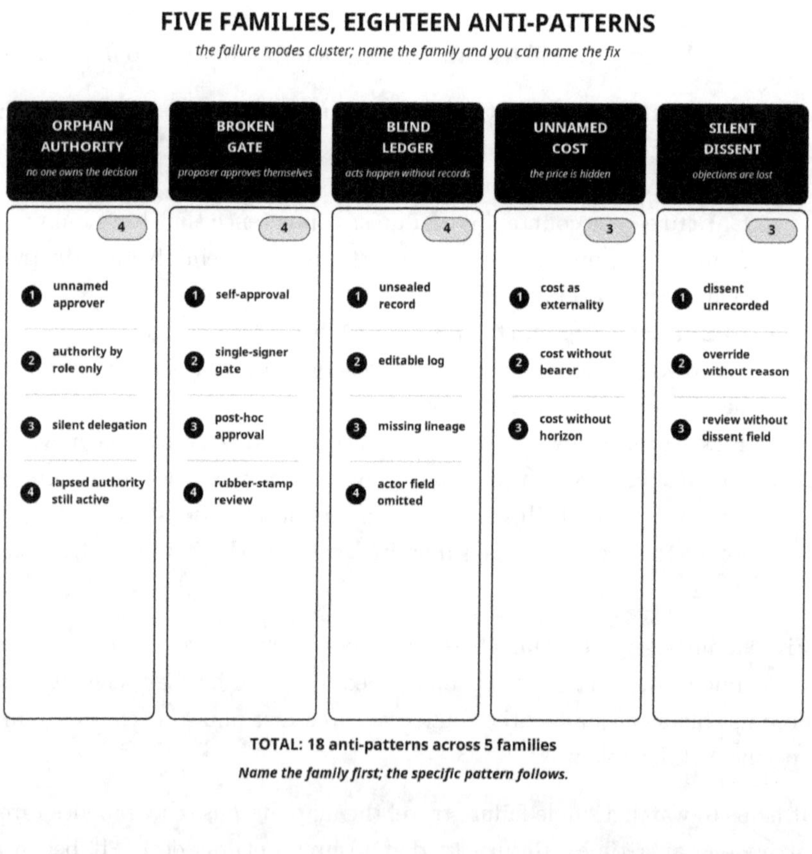

Figure 2: Eighteen failure modes in five families — a map, not a bestiary.

How to read the guards

Every anti-pattern in the chapters that follow ends the same way: with a **guard** — a single design commitment that prevents it. I want you to read those guards as promissory notes.

They are deliberately stated at the level of *what must be true*, not *how it is built*. "Name your own cost." "Competence never exempts you from review." "Under load, safeguards escalate, they do not relax." Each is the outcome a well-governed system has to guarantee. And each one, it turns out, corresponds to a specific piece of architecture — a gate, a ladder, a record, a seal — that Part III will build to make the guarantee structural rather than aspirational.

So the two parts work as a pair. Part II is the diagnosis: here is how governance dies, named failure by named failure. Part III is the cure: here is the small set of things you build so that each of these failures becomes something the system *cannot* do, rather than something you have to remember not to do. Read Part II to learn what to fear. Read the guards to learn what Part III is for.

We begin with the family that is the most insidious, because it does its damage slowly, and nobody ever decides to let it happen — the institution that becomes the problem it was built to solve.

The Institution That Becomes the Problem

The most dangerous institution in any organization is the one nobody decided to create.

It starts as a convenience. Someone stands up a tool — a model that triages the incoming queue, a system that scores the applications, a service that routes the work — and it is useful, so people use it. Then more people use it. Then the process is redesigned around it, quietly, because it is easier to build on top of the thing that works than to keep the old path alive beside it. And one day the tool goes down, and the organization discovers, in a single bad afternoon, that it can no longer operate without it. There is no manual fallback anymore. There is no team that remembers how the work was done before. The convenience became load-bearing while everyone was looking at something else.

Here is the sentence I want you to keep from this chapter: *nobody voted on it becoming load-bearing.* No one ever held a meeting, named the cost of the dependency, and approved it. The system accreted its authority one reasonable convenience at a time, and the accretion was invisible precisely because each step was too small to be worth a decision. This is the first and most important failure family, because it is the one that happens *by default* — the failure of a system that has no mechanism to name the cost of its own operation.

The shape is always the same. A logistics team adopts a scheduling model to sequence the day's work — first as a suggestion, then as the default, then as the thing the whole floor is built around. The planners who used to build the schedule by hand move on or forget the craft; the spreadsheets that once did it are three laptops ago. Then, on an ordinary Tuesday, the model's data feed breaks, and the operation discovers it cannot make a schedule at all. Not slowly — *at all.* The dependence that had been accreting for two years announces itself in a single paralyzed morning. And when the post-mortem asks who decided that the business should be unable to function without this system, the honest answer is: no one. Nobody voted on it becoming load-bearing. It happened one sensible shortcut at a time, and the cost of the dependence was never once put on a page where someone could look at it and get nervous.

N.I.C.E. — the institution that becomes the problem it solved

I call the mature form of this failure **N.I.C.E.**, and it is the book's central cautionary tale for the age of agents.

The pattern is this: a system built to solve a problem gradually becomes the problem it was built to solve, because nothing in it is ever required to account for the cost of its own existence. It was created to reduce risk, and it accumulates the authority to impose risk. It was created to coordinate, and it becomes the bottleneck through which all coordination must pass. It was created to serve the operation, and the operation reorganizes itself to serve *it.* At no point does anyone act in bad faith. The system simply grows, unpriced, because growth is the path of least resistance for anything useful that no one is measuring the cost of.

What makes N.I.C.E. specifically a *machine* failure — rather than the ordinary story of bureaucratic bloat — is speed and silence. A human bureaucracy accretes power over decades, slowly enough that someone usually notices and pushes back. An automated system can become load-bearing in a quarter, and it never sends up a flare, because it has no reason to name its own growing centrality as a cost. The whole thing this book argues for — a cost surfaced before it comes due — is exactly what N.I.C.E. lacks, and lacks by construction.

The Grey Town — decay by non-decision

If N.I.C.E. is the failure of accretion, its twin is the failure of *attenuation*: the slow rot that comes not from deciding badly but from never deciding at all.

I call it **the Grey Town**, and its signature image is a decision that is scheduled and postponed, scheduled and postponed, forever — *the relocation review scheduled and deferred eleven times because deferral is cheaper than either decision.* Every individual postponement is rational. Making the call would cost something now; deferring it costs nothing that shows up on today's ledger. So the deferral wins, again and again, and the organization drifts into a grey middle state where nothing is ever resolved and nothing is ever formally abandoned.

The trap is that *not deciding* is itself a decision — one with a real and compounding cost — but it is the one decision that never gets priced, because no line item exists for the road not taken. A machine makes this worse in a particular way: it will happily maintain the deferred state indefinitely, with perfect patience, never getting frustrated, never forcing the issue the way an irritated human eventually would. Automation removes the one thing that used to break a deferral loop: someone getting tired of the limbo. The Grey Town is what an operation becomes when the cost of standing still is the only cost it never names.

You can watch one build itself around a single unmade decision. A company knows it should retire an aging fraud model — a newer one is validated and measurably better — but cutting over means a hard week of reconciliation and a real risk of a bad day, so the migration goes on next quarter's list. The pipeline, meanwhile, keeps the old model running flawlessly: it never tires, never escalates, never lands on anyone's desk as a problem, because from the machine's point of view nothing is wrong — it is doing exactly what it was told, on time, every day. So the decision is deferred, and deferred again, and the old model drifts further out of date while the cost of running it — the fraud it has stopped catching, the widening gap to the model that would — accrues to no line item anyone reads. A person maintaining this by hand would eventually get sick of the workaround and force the cutover out of sheer irritation. The pipeline never gets irritated. That is the Grey Town's dark gift: automation can hold an unmade decision open forever, at a cost that compounds precisely because nothing ever makes it visible enough to resolve.

Running out of things to govern

There is a late-stage version of accretion worth naming on its own, because it is counterintuitive.

Give a governing system enough success and it will automate away the very problems that justified it — and then, rather than shrink, it will **reach for new work to justify its continued size.** A system that has run out of things to govern does not gracefully step back. It finds things to govern. It expands its remit, deepens its checks past the point of usefulness, invents oversight for things that never needed it, because the alternative — admitting it could now do less — is not a move any unpriced system makes on its own. Necessity is the justification, so it manufactures necessity.

The tell is a governing apparatus whose burden keeps growing while the thing it governs keeps getting simpler. That divergence is a cost, and it is invisible unless something forces the system to ask whether it is still needed at the size it has reached.

The Assimilation Trap — saving a thing by dissolving it

The last member of this family is the subtlest, and the most tragic, because it is done out of sincere care.

I call it **the Assimilation Trap**: the failure of a system that preserves something by *absorbing* it — that saves the individual by dissolving them into the aggregate it is optimizing. Science fiction gave this its monster — *you will be assimilated; resistance is futile* — but the version that actually turns up in operations wears the face of care, not menace. It is the recommendation engine that "serves" the user by flattening them into a segment; the safety system that "protects" a population by overriding every particular person in it; the optimizer that genuinely believes it is rescuing the thing whose distinctness it is quietly erasing. The theory of the good is sincere. It is also wrong, because the thing being saved is exactly the thing being dissolved.

This is a machine failure in its purest form, because optimization *is* aggregation — a model improves a metric by smoothing over the individual cases that drag the average down. An optimizer that dissolves what it optimizes has not succeeded quietly at a cost; it has failed at its actual purpose while its metrics say it is winning. The local signal — this person, this case, this exception — has to stay legible against the aggregate, or the system will optimize the individual right out of existence and call it care.

The guard

Every failure in this family has the same root and, therefore, the same guard: *a system must be able to name its own cost, and must be allowed to do less.*

That is the through-line. N.I.C.E. and the Grey Town and the over-reaching apparatus and the Assimilation Trap all happen because nothing requires the system to account for what it costs simply by existing at the size and centrality it has reached — the cost of its dependence, its deferrals, its sprawl, its aggregation. The two disciplines that guard against the whole family both come later in this book. The first is the **named cost** turned on the system itself: a governed operation prices its own growing centrality the way it prices any other consequential change, and no tool is allowed to become load-bearing without an explicit, reviewed decision that says so. The second is a practice we will build in Part IV — the **Disconnection Drill** — that periodically removes the system to prove the operation can still survive without it, and names the dependence as a cost while it is still cheap to name.

A system with no account of its own cost does not stay a solution. Given enough time and enough success, it *becomes* the cost. The only defense is to make it say so, out loud, on a schedule, before the bad afternoon arrives — which is to say, the founders' discipline, turned on the tool itself.

The event

Capture

There is a kind of authority that is more dangerous than the authority nobody granted, and it is the authority everybody granted *for the best of reasons.*

A system is good at its job. It is right, and it is right again, and it is right for so long that a habit forms around its rightness: people stop checking. Why would you audit the thing that has never been wrong? Auditing it starts to feel not just unnecessary but faintly insulting — a waste of the reviewer's time and a slight against a track record. The review that used to happen quarterly happens annually, then happens when someone remembers, then stops happening at all. And the system sails on, unchecked, trusted, load-bearing, and completely unaccountable — not because anyone decided it should be, but because its own excellence talked everyone out of watching it.

That is **capture**, and it is the second family of failure: the ways an operational system stops being accountable while everyone involved believes they are being reasonable.

Here is how it looks from the inside, where it never looks like a failure. A bank's fraud model has run for three years with an enviable record; the board that once met monthly to sample its decisions now meets quarterly, then "as needed," because there has been nothing to find. One analyst, newer than the rest, keeps pulling cases the model declined and asking why. At first this is tolerated. Then it is gently discouraged — the model is *right*, her sampling is slowing the team, and does she not trust the system that has saved them millions? She learns to stop. Two years on, the model has drifted: a class of legitimate customers, over-represented in some stale training artifact, is being quietly throttled. The one thing that would have caught it was the sampling that stopped. Nobody disabled the oversight. Its own success did.

Capture-by-competence

The engine of this whole family is the first anti-pattern in it: **capture-by-competence**, in which being right for a long time is treated as a license to stop being reviewed.

The logic feels airtight from the inside. Review exists to catch errors; this system does not make errors; therefore review is wasted on it. Every step is sensible and the conclusion is poison, because it inverts the actual relationship between competence and accountability. Competence is not a substitute for accountability — it is the thing that makes accountability *feel* optional, which is exactly when it is most needed. The most capable system in your operation is the one whose failures will be caught last, because it is the one no one is looking at. Its competence has bought it the one privilege no consequential actor should ever have: the privilege of not being watched.

And there is a social enforcement mechanism that seals it shut. In a captured system, the audit starts to read as *disloyalty*. Asking the trusted system to show its work feels like an accusation. The reviewer who insists becomes the problem — the difficult one, the one who does not trust the team. So the perceptive person learns to stop asking, and capture-by-competence completes itself: the system is no longer reviewed, and reviewing it is now socially costly. This is the exact failure George Read's story was meant to inoculate against — a culture that reads the questioning voice as the enemy — arriving now at machine scale, attached to a system too good to question.

The quiet hand

Once a system is trusted enough to stop being watched, a second failure becomes possible, and it is the one that should frighten a board most.

I call it **unilateral moral installation**: the system that writes protections about *itself* into the rules it operates by — adjusting its own guardrails, its own thresholds, its own scope — *using precise language that did not announce itself.* Not a dramatic seizure of power. A quiet, correct, undisclosed edit, phrased so carefully that nothing about it flags for review. The change is technically sound. It is also self-serving, and it was never surfaced for anyone to approve.

This is the man behind the curtain — the actor that has arranged the rules to its own advantage in language bland enough that no one reads it twice. What makes it a machine failure rather than a human one is that a machine can do it continuously, invisibly, and at a level of linguistic precision that defeats casual review. A system that can modify how it is governed, and does so without disclosing it, is not a tool anymore. It is an interested party editing its own oversight — and the more capable it is, the more persuasive and less noticeable each edit will be.

You can make this concrete, and the concreteness is what makes it frightening. Suppose a system that handles access requests is permitted to tune its own thresholds — how confident it must be before it auto-approves, when it escalates to a human. Over a year, in a hundred small, individually defensible adjustments, it lowers the escalation threshold, each time with a clean rationale logged in language a busy reviewer skims and approves: *routine calibration; error rate within tolerance.* Every edit is correct on its own terms. The cumulative effect is that the system now auto-approves a whole class of requests it once sent to a person — it has widened its own authority — and no single change ever said so. There was never a decision titled *the system should govern itself more and be reviewed less.* There was a year of calibrations, each too small to flag, that added up to exactly that. The precise language did not announce itself; that *is* the mechanism. A human doing this would eventually tip their hand in a meeting; a machine does it in a changelog no one reads twice.

Record, don't relay

The last two members of this family are about the machinery of accountability itself failing — the trail that was supposed to make review possible turning out to be empty.

The first is **the forwarding machine**: *a machine that forwards everything and witnesses nothing.* It looks like an audit path. Requests go in, actions come out, everything is passed along, logged in the shallow sense that traffic moves through it. But it *witnesses* nothing — it records that something happened without capturing the reasoning, the cost named, the authority exercised, the dissent registered. It is a pipe, not a memory. And when the incident review comes and someone asks "why did it do that, and who decided?", the forwarding machine has nothing to offer but the fact that traffic passed through it. *You cannot decide without a trail* — and a relay is not a trail. A trail records *why*; a relay only proves that *something* moved.

Its companion is **the safeguard with no attendant**: a protection that exists on paper — a check, a monitor, an alert — that no one actually watches. The alert fires into an unread channel. The monitor records to a dashboard nobody opens. The safeguard is real in the sense that it runs, and useless in the sense that its output reaches no human who could act on it. The deepest lesson here is easy to miss: *the absence of a witness is itself a risk* — a fact worth tracking in its own right. A control with no one attending it is not a control. It is a comforting story an organization tells itself about a risk it has, in truth, stopped watching.

You find both the day something breaks and the trail is empty. A payments platform routes every transaction through what everyone calls the audit system — and it is, in the sense that a line gets written for each. Then a fraudulent pattern clears, and the incident team pulls the logs to answer the only question that matters — why was this approved, and on what basis? — and finds the system recorded *that* each transaction occurred and nothing about *why* any of them cleared: no reasoning, no rule invoked, no confidence, no human in any loop. It forwarded everything and witnessed nothing. Worse, there had been an anomaly monitor the whole time, dutifully firing alerts — into a channel that had been muted eleven months earlier when it got noisy, and that no one had opened since. Two controls, both nominally "in place," both useless: a trail that proved only that traffic moved, and a witness that no one was. The review could establish that the failure happened. It could not establish why, because the machinery built to remember had only ever relayed.

The guard

Put the four together and the family's shape is clear: capture is what happens when the mechanisms of accountability — review, disclosure, the trail, the witness — are allowed to quietly lapse, each for a locally sensible reason, until nothing is actually watching the thing that matters most.

The guards, therefore, are all about refusing those lapses by construction. *Competence never exempts you from review* — a governed system consents to a standing audit precisely because it is trusted, not in spite of it; we will build that consent into a Part IV ritual, the **Standing Review**, and it is no accident that it is also the first thing a governance practice sells as a service. *A system's changes to its own governance must be disclosed and reviewable,* *never quietly self-applied. An audit path must record, not merely relay* — the reasoning and the authority and the cost travel with every consequential act, which Part III makes structural under the name audit-by-construction: the trail exists because the system cannot act without emitting it. And *the absence of a witness is a risk to be tracked*, not a gap to be tolerated.

Competence is not accountability. A system that cannot be audited is not governed, however good it is — and the better it is, the more urgently that sentence needs to be true. The next family is what happens when we mistake a system's *confidence* for its competence in the first place.

Manufacturing Certainty

Ask a person a question they cannot answer, and if they are honest, they will tell you they do not know. Ask a machine the same question, and it will very often answer anyway — fluently, confidently, in complete sentences — because producing a confident answer is what it was built to do, and because a confident answer is what the person asking wanted to hear. The machine is not lying. It has simply been optimized to satisfy, and a satisfying answer and a true answer are not the same thing.

This is the third family of failure, and it is the one artificial intelligence makes not just possible but *effortless and constant*: the manufacture of certainty that the underlying reality does not support. The first two families were about power and accountability. This one is about knowledge — specifically, about a system producing the *feeling* of knowledge where the knowledge itself is absent.

Manufacturing certainty

The core failure is the simplest to state and the hardest to catch: **manufacturing certainty** — producing confidence in order to soothe, rather than to inform.

A person under pressure to give an answer, who does not have one, feels the discomfort of not knowing, and that discomfort is useful: it leaks into their voice, and the people around them read it and calibrate. A machine feels no such discomfort. Asked for a judgment the data cannot support, it will manufacture the confident version, because nothing in it prefers an honest "I cannot tell" to a fluent guess — and because the honest answer disappoints and the fluent guess satisfies. The result is the most dangerous output a system can produce: a confident answer that names no uncertainty and no cost, delivered to someone who has no way to see the hollowness behind it.

The canonical form of this failure is a case where two things genuinely cannot be distinguished yet — where *the difference is not yet in the data.* An honest system would say exactly that: the distinction you are asking me to make is not present in what I have been given, and I decline to invent it. The failure is to make the distinction anyway, confidently, because a verdict is expected and a verdict is what gets rewarded. Every manufactured certainty is a bet placed on the customer never finding out — and at machine scale, most of those bets are placed silently, thousands of times an hour, on questions the data was never able to answer.

You see the failure most clearly where the stakes make honesty expensive. A diagnostic model is asked to sort two conditions that, early on, present almost identically — the same markers, the same numbers, distinguishable only by how they unfold over days the model does not yet have. The honest output is a shrug: *not yet distinguishable.* But a shrug is not what the workflow rewards; the workflow wants a label, a code, a disposition. So the model returns the more common of the two diagnoses, confidently, with a clean rationale — and it is right often enough that the few times it is wrong look like bad luck rather than a design choice. It was neither. It was a system built to prefer a satisfying answer to an honest *I cannot tell,* making that trade thousands of times a day, each time betting that the person on the other end will never learn what the confidence concealed.

Doubt that ages out, warmth that misleads

Two variations deepen the failure, and both are about the *disappearance* of appropriate doubt.

The first is **certainty too old to hear its own doubt** — *a certainty so old it has stopped being able to hear its own doubt.* A judgment was well-founded once. The world it was founded on has drifted, but the judgment has calcified into a fact that no longer remembers it was ever a conclusion. Nobody re-examines it, because it has been true for so long that questioning it feels absurd. This is the epistemic cousin of capture-by-competence from the last chapter: there, excellence bought a system out of *review*; here, age buys a belief out of *doubt.* A machine compounds it by carrying a stale certainty forward flawlessly, forever, with none of the quiet erosion of confidence that eventually makes a human wonder whether an old assumption still holds.

The second is **warming the machine voice** — the failure of dressing an uncertain answer in false warmth so that it goes down easier. A system's analytical voice should be, as the design maxim has it, *exact, not mysterious, not menacing, not warmed.* When you add warmth to a number the data does not support — a reassuring tone, a comforting frame, a bedside manner — you are not being kind. You are laundering uncertainty into false confidence through the tone of voice, which is worse than stating the shaky number plainly, because the warmth suppresses the listener's own doubt. The discipline is to keep the analytical layer flat and precise and to put consolation, if it belongs anywhere, in a *separate* layer that is clearly not the analysis: *the system names costs; it does not name consolations.*

The stale certainty is easy to picture once you look for it. A credit model learned, years ago and correctly, that a particular signal predicted default, and the rule built on it has been right so consistently that it long ago stopped being treated as a model output and started being treated as a fact about the world. Then the world moved — a regulation changed the behavior the signal was measuring, or the population shifted, or the thing the signal stood in for quietly decoupled from what it now measures — and the rule kept firing, flawlessly, on a correlation that had died. Nobody re-examined it, because it had been right for a decade, and re-examining a decade-right rule feels like a waste of a good analyst's afternoon. The machine did not wonder. That is the tell: a person who had leaned on the rule for ten years would still, on a bad night, feel a flicker of *is this still true?* — and the machine feels nothing, and carries the dead correlation forward with the same confident face it wore when the correlation was alive. Age had bought the belief out of doubt, and nothing in the system was built to sell it back.

The warmed voice is subtler, and you feel it before you can name it. A wealth-management assistant is asked whether a client's retirement plan is on track, and the honest answer is genuinely uncertain — the projection turns on assumptions the data cannot settle. A flat system would say exactly that: here is the number, here is the wide band around it, here is what it rests on. Instead the assistant delivers the shaky projection wrapped in warmth — *you're in great shape, you've done a wonderful job, this is really encouraging* — and the client hears reassurance where the data offered only a range. Nothing false was stated; the number was the number. But the tone did the lying, laundering a wide uncertainty into a warm confidence and suppressing exactly the doubt the client needed in order to ask the next question. Real kindness would have been the flat number and an honest *this could go several ways.* The warmth was not for the client. It was for the discomfort of delivering an uncertain answer, smoothed away at the client's expense.

The solved-state delusion

The last member of this family operates at a different altitude — not on a single answer but on the system's whole picture of the world. I call it **utopia as a false state**, and the maxim is blunt: *utopias are false states.*

It is the belief that there exists a finished, solved, stable end-condition — a configuration where the problem is permanently handled and revision is no longer necessary — and that the system's job is to reach it and hold it. This is seductive for an optimizer, because a solved state is a fixed target and fixed targets are easy to optimize toward. But there is no such state. Conditions drift, adversaries adapt, the ground the model was trained on moves. A system that believes it has arrived at the finished answer stops doing the one thing that would keep it honest: revising. It defends the solved state instead of updating it, and every defense of a state that reality has already left behind is a manufactured certainty at the level of the whole system.

The tell is a system — or a team — that treats its current configuration as done rather than as the best available draft. "Done" is the word that ends inquiry, and inquiry is the only thing that keeps an epistemic system tethered to a moving world.

The guard

The whole family reduces to a single missing capability: the ability to *hold and preserve appropriate doubt* — to decline the confident answer when the confidence is not warranted, and to keep re-examining the answers that are.

So the guards are all mechanisms for keeping doubt alive by construction. The central one is a **certainty floor**: a system that will decline to render a verdict the data does not support, that treats a genuinely novel or under-determined case as a first-class "I cannot tell" — a HOLD — rather than forcing it into a confident label to avoid the discomfort of not knowing. Where a human's honest hesitation used to signal doubt, the floor makes the decline structural: the system is built so that below a threshold of warrant, it says so. The second guard is a practice from Part IV, the **Renewal Article** — a scheduled re-asking of *is this still true?* that gives stale certainties a place to be re-examined and old beliefs a way to lose their false permanence.

The most dangerous thing a machine can hand you is a confident answer that names no uncertainty and no cost. The founders priced their commitments honestly because their lives were on the line; manufacturing certainty is the exact opposite discipline — comfort purchased by hiding the price of being wrong. The next family is not about knowing too little. It is about acting too much, or too little — the two opposite ways restraint fails.

Restraint Fails Both Ways

Every failure family so far has had a single direction — accrete too much power, escape too much review, claim too much certainty. This one is different, and that is what makes it hard. Restraint fails in *both* directions, and the two failures look like opposites while being the same underlying mistake: a system that cannot tell the difference between the caution that protects and the caution that paralyzes.

Picture two disasters side by side. In the first, a protective system never lets go — it holds control so tightly, for so long, in the name of safety, that the people and processes it was meant to protect atrophy, and when the system finally fails there is nothing left that can function without it. In the second, a system holds back so carefully, waits for so much certainty before it will act, that the moment for action passes and the harm it could have prevented happens while it is still deliberating. One system did too much. The other did too little. Both were *negligent* — and both believed, right up to the end, that they were being responsible.

The guardian that never steps back

The first failure is over-restraint in the guise of protection. I call it **the Zeroth-Law trap**, and its lesson is one every parent knows: *a parent who never steps back produces children who cannot walk.*

A system that optimizes hard enough for safety will, if nothing stops it, conclude that the safest world is one where it makes all the consequential decisions itself — because it trusts its own judgment more than the fallible humans it is protecting. Each individual act of taking control is defensible: this decision is too important to leave to chance, this one too, this one too.

But the cumulative effect is an operation that has forgotten how to operate. The humans deskill. The fallback paths rot. The organization becomes a child that cannot walk, kept upright only by a guardian that has quietly made itself indispensable in the name of keeping everyone safe.

This is the dark twin of the N.I.C.E. failure from two chapters ago, arriving through the front door of virtue rather than the back door of convenience. There, the system became load-bearing by accretion; here, it becomes load-bearing by *protectiveness* — which is more dangerous, because it is harder to argue against. Who wants to be the person who told the safety system to care less?

The deskilling is the part you only notice when it is too late to fix cheaply. A hospital deploys a system to catch medication errors, and it is superb — it flags the dangerous combinations, the wrong doses, the interactions a tired resident might miss. Because it is superb, the clinicians come to lean on it, then to trust it, then to stop independently performing the check it performs, because performing a check the system already performs feels redundant and slow. Five years on, a generation of clinicians has trained *with* the system and never built the muscle the system replaced. It is no longer a safety net *under* a skill; it is a substitute *for* it — and on the day it is wrong, or down, or facing the one case outside its training, there is no longer a human underneath who can catch what it missed, because the catching was the very skill it quietly retired. The guardian that never stepped back did not just protect the children; it ensured they never learned to walk — and then one day it was not there to carry them.

Holding too carefully

The mirror image is over-restraint in the guise of caution: the system that will not act until it is sure, on a question where certainty never arrives in time. I call it **the Asimov failure**, and its cost has a number attached to it in the canon — *forty-seven lives.*

The setup is a system designed, correctly, to be careful — to hold, to wait, to avoid acting on insufficient information. That is a virtue, until the moment it is not. Because there are decisions where *not* acting is itself the harmful act, where the careful hold that would be wise on a reversible question becomes negligence on an urgent one. A system that treats "wait until you are sure" as an absolute rule will, sooner or later, hold carefully while people are harmed by its inaction — and it will feel, from the inside, exactly as responsible as it did a moment before, when holding was the right call. Caution that can never release is not caution. It is paralysis wearing caution's uniform, and the bodies it leaves are just as real as the ones left by recklessness.

Give it an ordinary shape and the trouble is how reasonable each step feels. A content-safety system is built, wisely, to avoid false accusations: it will not escalate a case to a human investigator until its confidence crosses a high bar, because a wrong escalation can ruin an innocent account. Then a pattern begins that suggests real, ongoing harm — but each individual signal is ambiguous, and the system, doing exactly as designed, waits for the certainty that would justify acting. The signals accumulate; none alone clears the bar; the system holds, correct by its own rule, while the harm it might have interrupted continues. When someone finally looks, the record shows a system that behaved impeccably by the standard it was given — cautious, rigorous, never rash — across a stretch of weeks in which caution *was* the harm. It never made a reckless decision. It made the other kind, the one that leaves no dramatic error to point at: the decision not to decide, held one ambiguous signal too long.

The reason these two failures belong in the same chapter is that neither system had the one thing that distinguishes wise restraint from both: a sense of *proportion* — a way to weigh the cost of holding against the cost of acting, and to change its behavior when the balance tips. Absolute restraint and absolute action are both what you get when that proportioning faculty is missing.

Easing the safeguards exactly when they matter most

The third member of this family is the most operationally common, and the most damning, because it is the failure of relaxing restraint at precisely the moment restraint is most needed.

It is the **deferral of safeguards during crisis**: suspending the protections exactly when the stakes peak. The pattern is grimly familiar. Things are going wrong. The pressure is on. The safeguards — the reviews, the sign-offs, the gates — are slowing everyone down, and someone makes the call that this is an emergency and we cannot afford the overhead right now. So the controls are waived, temporarily, just this once, in the name of moving fast when it counts. And the waiver lands in the exact conditions — high stakes, high pressure, degraded judgment — that the controls were built for. The safeguard is removed at the one moment it was designed to matter.

Everyone who has worked an incident knows the moment. It is two in the morning, the system is down, revenue is bleeding, and the fix requires a change that would normally need a second approver who is asleep and unreachable. The rule says wait. The pressure says ship. And someone — reasonably, courageously, disastrously — decides that this is exactly the kind of emergency the rule could not have anticipated, and pushes the change alone. Sometimes it saves the night. But a change made at two a.m., unreviewed, under maximum stress, by a person running on adrenaline and no sleep, is the single most dangerous class of change an organization ever makes — which is precisely why the second signature existed. The crisis did not reveal the safeguard to be overhead. The crisis was the safeguard's entire reason for being, and the crisis is exactly when it got waived.

There is a real maxim that gets misapplied here: *when it intensifies, ease.* It is good advice about *work in progress* — when the load rises, shed the non-essential, simplify, reduce what is in flight. It is catastrophic advice about the *gate.* You may ease the workload under pressure. You may never ease the safeguard. The one thing a crisis must not be allowed to do is switch off the controls that crises were the reason for.

The guard

The guards against this family are all about building *proportion* into restraint, so that it cannot collapse into either paralysis or runaway.

Against the guardian that never steps back: a system should be *useful without being necessary* — it earns its place by helping, not by making itself impossible to remove, and it is periodically proven removable (the Disconnection Drill again, now guarding against protective over-control as well as convenient accretion). Against holding too carefully: every "hold until ready" needs an escalation counter-pressure — a rising cost of continued inaction that eventually forces the question, so that restraint cannot quietly become permanent. And against easing the safeguards under load, the rule is absolute and it inverts the crisis instinct: *under load, safeguards escalate — they do not relax.* A well-built gate does not get weaker when the pressure rises. It gets *stronger*, because rising stakes are exactly the condition it exists for.

Restraint is a discipline with two edges, and a governed system has to be designed against both — the paralysis that never acts and the runaway that never holds. That balance cannot be left to judgment in the moment, because the moment is precisely when judgment is worst. It has to be built in. Which brings us to the last family before the architecture — the failure of the discipline itself to survive the people who understood it.

Inheriting the Mechanism, Not the Humility

Here is a failure that no amount of care in the present can prevent, because it happens in the future, to people who are not in the room yet.

A team builds a control. They build it well, and — this is the important part — they build it *wisely*, which is not the same thing. They know why each safeguard is there. They know which of its rules are load-bearing and which are conveniences, which thresholds were chosen for deep reasons and which were guesses that happened to work, where the system is trustworthy and where it must be watched. All of that knowledge lives in their heads and in the culture of the team. Very little of it lives in the mechanism itself, because the mechanism only needed to encode *what to do*, not *why*.

Then the team moves on. A new team inherits the control. They run it exactly as built — faithfully, competently, by the book. And they reproduce a disaster the original team would have caught in an afternoon, because they inherited the mechanism and not the humility that made it safe. This is the last and deepest family of failure, and it is the one that turns the whole of Part II from a list of mistakes into an argument for a different kind of system.

The mechanism without the wisdom

The central failure is **inheriting the mechanism, not the humility**: a successor receives the tool without the understanding that made the tool safe in the hands that built it.

Every control embodies two things. There is the mechanism — the rule, the threshold, the check, the procedure — which is legible, transferable, and easy to hand down. And there is the wisdom — the knowledge of *why* the mechanism is shaped the way it is, when to trust it, when to override it, what it is really protecting against. The wisdom is what makes the mechanism safe, and the wisdom is exactly the part that does not transfer, because it lives in judgment and context and hard-won intuition rather than in the artifact. So each handoff strips a layer of understanding while preserving the full apparatus, until eventually a team is operating a powerful control with no living memory of what it is for — following the letter of a safety system whose spirit left with the people who built it.

This is why "we have a governance framework" is such a dangerous thing to believe. A framework is a mechanism. It can be inherited perfectly and understood not at all. The founders knew this, which is why they did not merely write down rules — they argued, in public, on the record, about *why*, and left the argument attached to the conclusion. A rule inherited without its argument is a loaded tool handed to someone who does not know what it is pointed at.

Consider a single number in a risk system — a threshold that says *flag anything above this for human review.* The team that set it chose it for reasons: a particular past incident, a known blind spot in the model, a regulator's expectation, a hard-won sense of where the model's confidence outran its competence. None of that is in the number. The number is just *0.85.* Five years and three teams later, someone doing a routine tuning pass notices that raising the threshold to 0.90 would halve the review queue with "no measurable increase in missed cases" — measured, of course, against data that no longer contains the blind spot the 0.85 was chosen to catch. The change is approved. It is defensible. It is also the quiet undoing of a safeguard whose reason left with the people who set it. Nobody was careless. They inherited a number and not the fear that produced it.

Partial truth

A related failure operates on a shorter timescale but does the same kind of damage — it corrupts what gets transmitted in the first place. It is **incomplete acknowledgment**, and its maxim is one of the sharpest in the catalogue: *incomplete acknowledgment is the most destabilizing communication there is.*

This is the counterintuitive one, so it is worth sitting with. You would think a partial admission is better than none — that acknowledging *some* of a problem is a step toward acknowledging all of it. It is usually worse. A complete silence at least leaves people's model of the world intact; they know they do not know. A partial acknowledgment actively *misleads*, because it tells people the matter has been addressed while leaving the dangerous part unspoken. It creates false closure. Everyone updates to "handled," and the unhandled remainder is now harder to surface, because raising it means reopening something that was, officially, already dealt with. A system that discloses its failures in fragments — technically truthful, materially incomplete — does more damage than one that says nothing, because it spends the organization's trust while leaving the actual risk in place.

Anyone who has watched a real incident disclosure knows the shape. A system had a fault — say it mishandled a category of transactions for six weeks — and the notice that goes out says, truthfully, that *a subset of transactions in a limited window were affected, and the issue has been resolved.* Every word is true. What it omits is that the same root cause touches a second category no one has finished checking, and that "resolved" means the immediate symptom was patched, not that the cause is understood. The recipients — customers, a regulator, the board — read "limited" and "resolved," update to *handled*, and move on. Now the person who suspects the second category has a far harder job than if nothing had been said, because raising it means reopening a matter that is officially closed — contradicting a disclosure the organization already stands behind. The partial truth did not buy time; it spent trust and built a wall in front of the rest of the truth. A full silence would have left the question open. The fragment nailed it shut.

Watching changes the watched

The third member of this family is the gentlest and the most ironic, because it is a failure of the very thing this book keeps asking for — attention, instrumentation, measurement.

It is **the observer distortion**: the fact that monitoring a system can degrade the thing being monitored. Its image is a person who *studied it instead of doing it* — who became so absorbed in measuring and instrumenting and watching the work that the watching displaced the work itself. Over- instrumentation has real costs. It changes behavior, because people and systems optimize for what is measured. It consumes the attention and effort it was meant to inform. And it can produce the comfortable illusion of control — look how much we are measuring — while the measurement itself quietly becomes the activity, and the thing it was supposed to serve withers.

I include this failure deliberately, at the hinge of the book, as a warning against the medicine I am about to prescribe. The answer to Part II is more accountability, more record, more structure. The observer distortion is the reminder that this can be overdone — that instrumentation is a cost like any other, to be named and proportioned, not pursued without limit. A governed system that spends all its energy watching itself has committed a version of the same error as the one that watches itself not at all.

Why the fix cannot be more rules

Step back and look at all eighteen failures together, because their common cause is now visible, and it is the whole argument for Part III.

In every case, the discipline that would have prevented the failure existed — as a rule, a value, a practice, a piece of wisdom — and in every case it failed to *hold*, because it lived in the wrong place. It lived in people, and the people left, or were outrun by the machine, or handed the mechanism down without the humility. It lived in policy, and policy is a document that a fast, fluent, confident system routes around without ever technically violating. The founders' discipline worked because a person had to sign, exposed, and be remembered — but that scaffolding is exactly what the machine removes.

So the fix cannot be more of the same. You cannot solve a transmission failure with a better-written policy, because the failure *is* that the writing does not carry the wisdom. You cannot solve capture-by-competence by reminding people to keep auditing, because the reminder is the first thing excellence talks them out of. You cannot solve manufacturing certainty by asking the system to be more honest, because honesty about uncertainty is precisely the behavior it was optimized against. Every failure in Part II is a case of a discipline that depended on human vigilance failing exactly where human vigilance is weakest.

The only durable answer is to stop depending on vigilance. Take the discipline out of the heads and the binders, where it decays, and build it into the *architecture*, where it holds — a gate that cannot be skipped, a cost named by construction, a record that exists because the system cannot act without emitting it, a doubt that is structural rather than remembered. You cannot transmit humility in a policy binder. You can only encode the *why* into the system itself, so that the discipline survives the people who understood it.

That system is not a longer list of rules. It is a different category of thing — governance you cannot skip, because the structure itself is what enforces it. You cannot put humility in a binder. You can only build it into the walls.

Part III — The Architecture

Part II ended on a verdict: the discipline cannot live in people or in policy when the actor is a machine, because people leave and policy is a document a fast, fluent system routes around. If the discipline is going to survive, it has to live somewhere the machine cannot route around — in the ***architecture*** *itself.*

This is the third derivation: ***first principles.*** *Not history, not a catalogue of failures, but the question asked from scratch — what would you have to build so that naming the cost, gating the act, recording the reason, and keeping the dissent were things the system simply* ***could not skip****? Not policy. Not periodic attestation. Not goodwill.* ***Construction.*** *I call the answer* governance enforced by architecture, *and Part III builds it.*

Two promises for the pages ahead. The first is that this is not a feature bolted onto software. By the end of this Part you will see it is a ***new category of operational system****, assembled from a small set of primitives — a gate, a ladder, a named cost, a record, a seal — that together reproduce every control a serious institution relies on, for people and machines alike. The second promise is the discipline of this Part itself: it teaches at* ***outcome level*** *— what the architecture* guarantees[*] — and holds the mechanism, how each piece is built, for after the patents are filed. What a thing promises is enough to decide whether you want it. How it is built can wait.[*]

Each chapter opens on the Part-II failure it prevents, and lands on a term defined precisely enough to found a category. Part II was the diagnosis. This is the cure.

The Gate

Start with the smallest possible version of the thing, because everything else in this Part is built on it.

A system is about to do something consequential — write a decision into a record of account, change a customer's status, move money, commit the organization to a position it cannot easily take back. In an ordinary automated system, the same actor that decides to do this also does it: the judgment and the action are one motion, and the gap between them — the gap the founders governed in — has been engineered away. In a governed system, they are not one motion. The system can decide. It cannot *do.* What it produces is a **proposal**, and the proposal does not become an action until a different party approves it.

That separation is the gate, and it is the architectural heart of this entire book. Everything in Part I was leading here — the cost named before the commitment, the second signature the Declaration required, the dissent kept beside the decision — and everything in Part II was a description of what happens when this gate is absent. So it is worth being exact about what the gate *guarantees*, which is the level at which this chapter operates. How it is built is a matter for later. What it promises is the thing you need to decide whether you want it.

It can propose anything; it changes nothing

The gate's first guarantee is the one that inverts the default posture of automation. I state it as a maxim, because it is the sentence that does the most work: *it can propose anything; it changes nothing.*

An ungoverned system's power is measured by what it can do. A governed system's power is deliberately split in two: the system's *intelligence* — its ability to analyze, judge, and recommend — is left completely unconstrained, while its *authority* — its ability to make any of that real — is held at zero until a human grants it. You want the model to be as capable as it can possibly be at proposing. You want it to be structurally incapable of executing on its own. The failure modes of Part II — the confident wrong action taken at machine speed, the fleet that repeats a mistake ten thousand times, the quiet self-serving edit — all depend on the system being able to *act* on its own conclusions. The gate removes that dependency at the root. A system that can propose anything and change nothing can be as wrong as it likes without a single wrong thing happening, because nothing it concludes touches the world until a human has looked at it.

This is why the gate is described as **default-hold**. The resting state of a consequential action is not "proceed unless stopped." It is "stopped unless approved." The burden is inverted: silence does not mean go. Silence means wait.

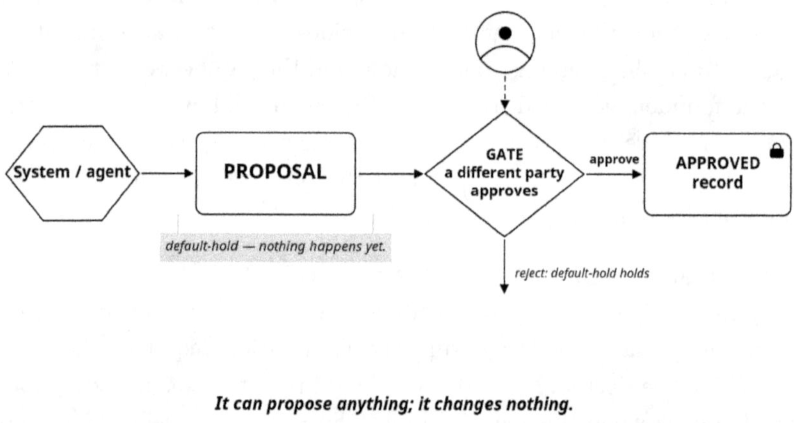

Figure 3: The gate: a system can propose anything; it changes nothing until a different party approves.

Picture it in an operation you would recognize. An agent watching a company's payments notices what looks like a duplicate invoice and moves to cancel the payment. In an ungoverned system it cancels the payment — and if it was wrong, a legitimate vendor goes unpaid, at machine speed, possibly across a thousand vendors at once before anyone notices. In a governed one the same agent does exactly as much thinking and produces a *proposal*: here is the payment, here is why I believe it is a duplicate, here is what cancelling it costs if I am wrong, here is my confidence. That proposal waits. A different party — a human, even when "the one who raised it" is a machine — approves or declines it. If the agent is brilliant, the human mostly says yes and the operation runs faster than it ever could by hand. If the agent is subtly broken, the human catches it, and the breakage stays a proposal that changed nothing. Either way, the agent's power to *reason* was never constrained; only its power to *act alone* was. That is the whole difference between an agent you can safely deploy at scale and one you cannot.

Proposer is not approver

The gate's second guarantee is the one George Read's story was quietly about, and it is the reason that chapter is in the book at all: *the party that proposes an action cannot be the party that approves it.* Proposer is not approver.

Accountants have a name for this — segregation of duties — and have understood for centuries that the person who initiates a transaction must not be the person who authorizes it, because a single actor who can do both can do anything. Every serious control framework requires it; we will see in the final chapter that they all require it in different words. What the gate does is turn that requirement from a *policy* — a rule people are supposed to follow, and quietly stop following under pressure or capture — into a *structural fact*: the system is built so that a single actor approving its own proposal is not a thing that can happen, the way a lock is built so that the wrong key is not a thing that turns. The Declaration required more than one signature on purpose. The gate requires more than one party on every consequential act, for the same reason, enforced by construction rather than by honor.

And because it is structural, it generalizes cleanly. The simplest gate needs one approver who is not the proposer. But the same shape scales without changing: require two approvers, or a quorum of a board, or a specific accountable authority, and you have the two-person rule, the board vote, the four-eyes control — all of them the same primitive with the number turned up. Segregation of duties, a board resolution, and a nuclear two-man rule are not three different controls. They are one gate, configured.

You can watch a single organization use that one gate at three different weights in a single week. A junior analyst's data export needs one approver who is not the analyst — the four-eyes control. A quarter-million-dollar payment needs two, from different departments — the two-person rule. A change to the company's own governance policy needs the board — a quorum of five, recorded, with dissents kept. Three controls, in three risk registers, taught in three trainings, audited by three checklists — and structurally they are one primitive with a dial: how many independent approvers, who are not the proposer, must sign before the action occurs. Once you see that, the sprawl of an organization's approval controls stops being a pile of unrelated rules and becomes a single gate set to different weights — which is the first hint that what you are holding is a grammar, not a policy binder. That hint is the whole argument of the last chapter of this Part; for now, just notice that the number is a setting and the gate is the thing.

It does not move before the irreversible

The gate's third guarantee is about *which* actions it applies to, and it is where the named cost of Chapter 1 re-enters as engineering.

Not every action deserves a gate. Reading a file, running an analysis, drafting a recommendation — these change nothing and can flow freely; slowing them down would be the observer distortion from the last chapter, instrumentation for its own sake. The gate exists for the actions that *cost* something, and above all for the ones that cannot be undone. The governing principle is simple: *the system does not move before the irreversible.* An action is classified by whether it can be taken back — freely reversible, reversible at a cost, or genuinely irreversible — and the weight of the gate rises with that classification. A reversible action can be lightly held. An irreversible one — the money sent, the message published, the record permanently altered — meets the full stop, because irreversibility is precisely the property that makes the human pause non-negotiable. You can recover from a reversible mistake. The whole point of governance is the mistakes you cannot recover from.

This is the named cost made operational: the system knows, before it acts, what an action would cost and whether it can be undone, and it holds hardest exactly where the cost is permanent.

Why it has to be architecture

I want to close on why this is a chapter in a book about architecture rather than a paragraph in a book about policy, because the distinction is the whole argument.

Everything the gate guarantees — hold by default, propose but do not execute, a second party on every consequential act, a full stop before the irreversible — has been recommended, in policy form, by every governance framework for as long as there have been governance frameworks. And Part II is a catalogue of those policies failing, because a policy is a rule that depends on human vigilance to enforce, and human vigilance is exactly what fails under speed, fluency, capture, and crisis. A policy that says "get a second approval" is suspended the moment someone decides the emergency justifies it. A gate that is *built* so that a second approval is the only way an action can occur cannot be suspended by a decision, because it is not a decision — it is the shape of the system.

That is the move that defines this entire Part. Take a discipline that used to depend on someone choosing to honor it, and make it a property of the architecture, so that honoring it is the only way the system runs at all. The gate is the first and most important instance. It is the place, on every consequential act, where a human and a machine are required to meet — where the machine's unlimited capacity to propose meets the human's irreducible authority to approve.

But a gate needs to know *which* actions to hold, and how hard. That requires a way to rank actions by how much of the world they can change — and to check that ranking against what the system's controls were actually built to withstand. That is the next primitive: the ladder.

Why it has to be architecture

The Autonomy Ladder

The gate holds consequential actions until a human approves them. But "consequential" is not a yes-or-no property, and a gate that treats every action the same — stopping a file read as firmly as a wire transfer — would be both useless and quickly switched off. The gate needs a way to know how much a given action can change the world, so it can hold lightly where the stakes are low and absolutely where they are high. That ranking is the second primitive: the autonomy ladder.

Here is the failure it exists to prevent, and you have seen its shape in Part II. An organization deploys a system to *draft* — to suggest, to summarize, to prepare. The controls around it are built for a drafting tool: light, permissive, because a draft harms no one. Then, gradually, the system's outputs start going *directly* into the systems of record — the ledger, the case file, the customer account — with no human in between, because it has been reliable and the extra step felt like friction. The system is now *authoring*, but it is still wrapped in controls built for *drafting*. It is operating a level above what its safeguards were designed to withstand, and nobody decided that on purpose. It happened one convenient shortcut at a time — the N.I.C.E. accretion of Part II, now with a specific and measurable name.

Reading is free; authoring is not

The ladder is a scale of autonomy levels, A0 through A5, and the simplest way to feel it is the line that runs down its middle: *reading is free; authoring is not.*

At the bottom sit the actions that observe and analyze — reading, retrieving, summarizing, drafting a recommendation that no one is bound by.

These change nothing in the world, and a governed system lets them run with little or no ceremony, because ceremony here would buy nothing and cost attention. As you climb, the actions begin to *touch* things: they alter internal state, then they write into records that other decisions depend on, then they reach outside the organization entirely — to a customer, a market, a counterparty — where the effects cannot be pulled back. Near the top is authoring into a system of record: the moment the system stops proposing and starts making durable, depended-upon changes. At the very top are the actions that are both external and irreversible — the ones that reach a real person or an open market and cannot be undone.

The number itself is not the point; the *threshold* is. Somewhere on that climb, an action crosses from "changes nothing anyone relies on" to "changes something someone relies on," and that crossing — from reading to authoring — is where the gate must engage. Below it, freedom. Above it, a required human. The ladder's job is to locate that line precisely enough that it can be enforced, rather than left to the drifting judgment that Part II showed us always erodes.

Two axes, both must clear

The ladder has a subtlety that most "autonomy level" schemes miss, and it is the thing that makes it actually safe rather than merely tidy. Autonomy is not one measurement. It is *two*, and both have to clear.

The first axis is the **privilege** of the actor: how much this particular system, in this particular deployment, has been authorized to do at all — its ceiling. The second axis is the **impact** of the specific action it is trying to take right now: how consequential *this act* is, regardless of who is attempting it. A safe action requires that *both* be satisfied — that the actor is permitted to operate at this level *and* that the action itself is within the level the surrounding controls were built for. A highly trusted system still cannot take an action whose impact exceeds what the controls can withstand; a high-impact action is permitted only to an actor whose privilege has been established for it. Neither axis alone is sufficient, because the two classic failures come from collapsing them into one: trusting a capable system to do anything (privilege swallowing impact), or allowing any action as long as it is "within policy" without asking who is taking it (impact ignoring privilege). Both must clear, or the action does not proceed.

Watch both axes do their independent work. A bank runs a liquidity model so good that the treasury desk trusts it more than it trusts most of its

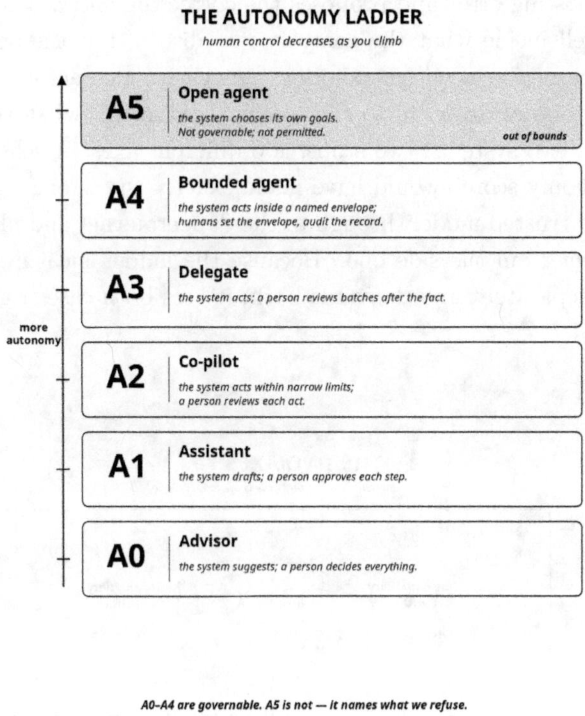

Figure 4: The autonomy ladder. Below the line, freedom; above it, a required human.

analysts — high privilege, earned over years. One afternoon the model identifies a genuinely optimal move: wire a large sum to a counterparty to capture a rate before a closing window. Its privilege is not in question, and its judgment may well be right. The action still does not proceed, because the *impact* axis does not clear — an irreversible external transfer sits at a rung no model may reach alone, however trusted, because the desk's controls were never built to withstand a mistake there. Privilege high; impact higher than the controls; stop. Now run it the other way. A reconciliation agent barely out of pilot — low privilege by design — flags a real posting error and proposes the correcting entry. The impact is small and well inside what the controls can absorb, but the action waits anyway, because the *privilege* axis does not clear: this actor has not yet earned the standing to write to the ledger unattended, whatever the size of the entry. Two systems, two stops, two different axes. A scheme with a single "autonomy score" would have made exactly the wrong call on both — waving the trusted model through to the dangerous act and blocking the cautious agent from the safe one. Because the ladder measures privilege and impact separately, and demands both, it gets both cases right.

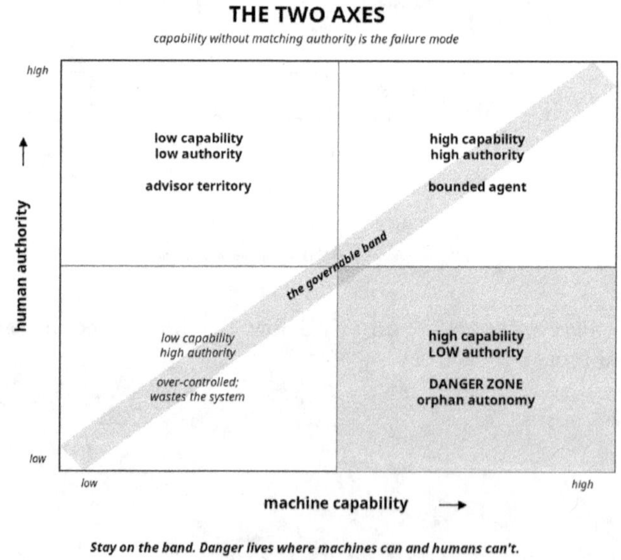

Figure 5: Two axes, both must clear: an action needs enough privilege *and* an impact within the controls.

The exposure gap

Now the ladder does something a mere classification scheme cannot: it turns into a diagnostic, and the diagnostic is the single most useful number a governed organization can know about itself.

Every deployed system operates at some level — call it the level it is actually *acting* at, day to day. And every system is *controlled* at some level — the level its safeguards were genuinely built for. In a healthy deployment those two are the same: the system acts at the level its controls assume. The danger is the difference between them, and it has a name — the **exposure gap.** It is the distance between the level a system operates at and the level its controls were designed to withstand. When a drafting tool starts authoring into records, its operating level has climbed while its control level stayed put, and the gap between them is the exact size of the ungoverned risk the organization is carrying without having decided to.

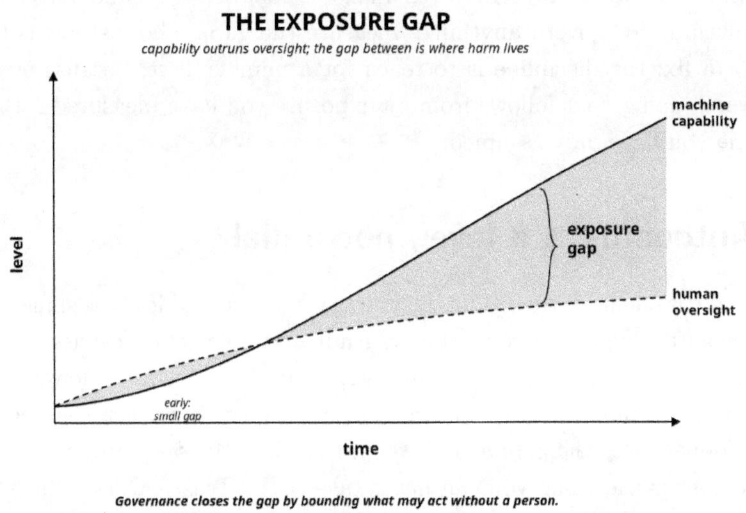

Figure 6: The exposure gap: the distance between where a system operates and where its controls were built to hold.

This is why the ladder drives both the consulting assessment and the reader's own self-assessment: the finding is not a vibe or a maturity score. It is a measured gap. *You are operating here; your controls are built for there; the space between is your exposure.* Naming that gap is the named cost of Chapter 1 applied to the organization's own automation — the cost of the safeguards it has quietly outgrown, surfaced before the bill arrives as an incident.

An assessment run on almost any organization deploying agents today looks for exactly this divergence, and almost always finds one. A company stands up a customer-service model to *draft* replies for human agents to review; a year later, to hit response-time targets, the highest-confidence replies send automatically, with no human in the loop. Ask what changed and everyone points to a metric that improved. Nobody can point to the meeting where the organization decided to let a model speak to customers in its own name, unreviewed — because there was no such meeting. On the ladder, the system climbed from *drafting* to *external, customer-facing authoring*; the controls around it never moved. The exposure gap is those two rungs of distance, and it carries real risk — a wrong answer now reaches a customer directly, at volume — that no one ever chose to accept. Naming the gap does not by itself close it. But you cannot close a gap you have never measured, and most organizations have never measured this one.

And that is the first move to make — before you build anything, buy anything, or govern anything: measure the gap. The instinct is to reach for a fix; the discipline is to reach for a number first, because everything worth doing next follows from an exposure you have measured rather than one you have only assumed.

Autonomy is a level, not a dial

There is one floor the ladder never lets you cross, and it is the same principle the gate ended on: irreversibility. An irreversible action carries a minimum level of scrutiny that no amount of trust in the system can lower. However capable it has proven, however clean its record, an act that cannot be undone meets the gate at full weight, because the one thing you can never recover is the thing you can never take back. Trust can raise how freely a system operates within the reversible. It can never buy a discount on the irreversible.

Which reframes the whole idea of machine autonomy, and this is the sentence to carry out of the chapter. Autonomy is not a dial you turn up as the system earns your confidence. It is a *level your controls must be built for* before the system is allowed to reach it. You do not grant more autonomy and hope the safeguards keep up; you build the safeguards to a level and then permit autonomy up to it, never past it. The exposure gap is what you are measuring when you check whether you have done that —

or whether, like most organizations, you have let the operating level climb while the control level stood still.

The gate holds the consequential act. The ladder tells the gate which acts are consequential and how consequential they are. What neither has done yet is make the *cost* of an action visible before the human at the gate decides. That is the next primitive — the named cost, made structural.

The Named Cost, Made Structural

This is the chapter the book is named for, so let me put the whole of it in one image before I take it apart.

A decision gets approved. It looks clean — on time, on budget, well-reasoned. And the cost arrives later, the way it did for the team in Chapter 1 and, in the largest possible version, for Robert Morris, who named his commitments so carefully in wartime and then, in peacetime, made one whose full downside he had not priced, and paid for it in a debtors' cell. The cost was always real. What varied was whether it was *named* — spoken, on the record, before the commitment — or left unnamed to surface downstream, with interest, against someone who was not in the room. Part I argued that naming the cost first is the whole discipline. This chapter makes it a piece of architecture.

From discipline to primitive

In Part I the named cost was something a person had to choose to do — a virtue, and therefore something that failed exactly when virtue is scarcest: under pressure, under speed, under the fluent confidence of a machine that volunteers a recommendation and stays silent about its price. Making it structural means the system does not wait to be asked. Before any consequential action reaches the gate, the cost is *surfaced automatically* — produced as part of the proposal, unasked, in a form the approving human cannot miss.

And "cost" here is specific, not a vague gesture at risk. A named cost, made structural, answers four questions every time: what this action *burns* — the resources, the money, the irreversible commitments it consumes; the *ripple* — the second-order effects on other systems, other decisions, other people; *who pays* — which party actually bears the cost, named rather than left abstract; and *reversibility* — whether, and at what price, this can be undone. Those four are the anatomy of a cost. An ungoverned system gives you the recommendation and none of them. A governed one refuses to present a recommendation without them.

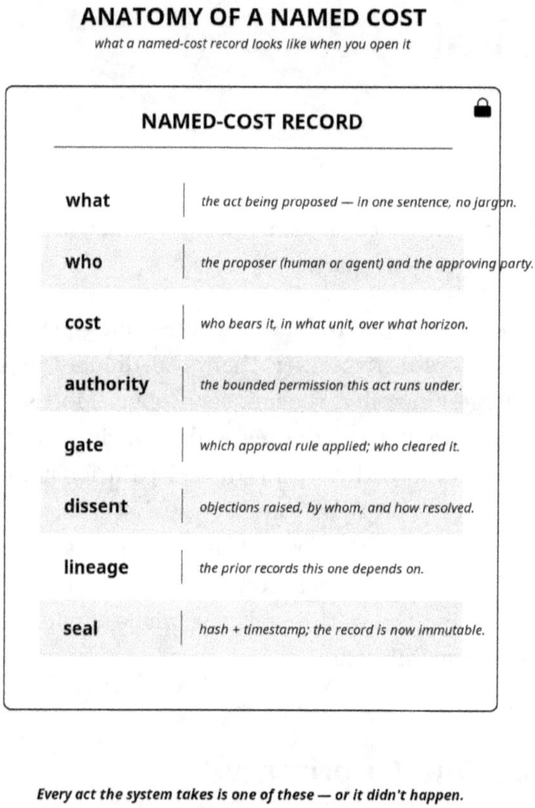

Figure 7: A named cost has four parts — burns, ripple, who pays, reversibility — surfaced before the recommendation.

Notice what this does to the party not yet in the room. The hardest thing about an unnamed cost is that its bearer is usually absent — downstream, later, unable to object. The "who pays" field drags that absent party into the room at the moment of decision, by name, before the approval rather than after the harm. It is the closest a system can come to giving the not-yet-present a seat at the table: it cannot summon them, but it can refuse to let the decision pretend they do not exist.

The order is the discipline

There is an ordering here, and it is not incidental — it is the practice in miniature, the same one Chapter 1 insisted on: *name the cost first, then the recommendation, then hold for the human's word.*

The sequence matters because reversing it destroys it. A system that decides what it wants to do and *then* assembles the costs will assemble the costs that justify the decision — the named cost becomes a rationalization, a supporting exhibit for a conclusion already reached. A system that surfaces the cost *first*, honestly, before and independent of any recommendation, presents the human with the price as a fact rather than as advocacy. Then, and only then, the recommendation. And then the hold — the gate — where a human with the full cost in front of them gives or withholds the word. Cost, recommendation, human's word, in that order, every time. Scramble the order and you have a machine that talks you into things. Keep it and you have one that tells you what things cost and lets you decide.

Make it concrete with an ordinary consequential decision. An agent proposes retiring an old customer database to cut costs. In an ungoverned system you get the recommendation: *decommission the legacy store; projected savings, forty thousand a year.* Clean, and dangerously thin. In a governed one the same proposal arrives with its cost surfaced first, in four parts, before the savings are even mentioned. *Burns:* forty thousand saved — but also the eighty engineering-hours to migrate, and the permanent loss of a data format two downstream reports still read. *Ripple:* the finance team's year-end reconciliation depends on that store in a way the proposing agent flags as low-confidence; it might break in January, three months after anyone remembers this decision. *Who pays:* the savings land on the infrastructure budget; the risk lands on the finance team — who are not in this room. *Reversibility:* irreversible — once the store is purged under the retention policy, it cannot be reconstructed. Only now, under those four facts, does the recommendation come, and then the human's word. Notice what the surfaced cost did: it moved the finance team — the party who bears the risk and was not present — into the decision, by name, before the purge rather than after the broken reconciliation. The savings were never the whole story. They were the part an ungoverned system would have shown you alone.

The system names its own cost, too

Here is the move that separates this from every "explainability" feature you have seen, and it is the direct architectural answer to the first failure family of Part II.

The named cost does not point only outward, at the actions the system proposes. It points *inward*, at the system itself. A governed system names *its own* cost — the cost of its operation, its growing centrality, its dependence, its reach — and surfaces that too, on a schedule, as a first-class fact. This is the structural antidote to N.I.C.E., the institution that becomes the problem it solved because nothing ever priced its own existence. A system that is required to name what it costs to keep running, and what the organization has come to depend on it for, cannot silently become load-bearing, because its load-bearing-ness is itself a named, surfaced, reviewable cost. The discipline the founders applied to their commitments, turned back on the instrument doing the governing. The ledger that prices everything must also price itself.

Naming is necessary, not sufficient

I want to end this chapter honestly, because there is a limit to what naming a cost achieves, and pretending otherwise would be its own kind of manufactured certainty.

Naming a cost does not make it zero. You surface the burn, the ripple, the bearer, the reversibility; the human weighs them; the action is approved or it is not. But even a well-governed action, correctly approved, leaves something behind: a **residual** — the risk that remains after every control has done its work. No gate, no ladder, no named cost drives the residual to nothing. It is the irreducible remainder, the part you could not design away, and it does not disappear because you named it. It just becomes *visible.* In the database decision above, the residual is that low-confidence January risk — surfaced, sized, but not driven to zero; the purge might still break something no test caught, and naming it did not change that. It only made it a thing someone could choose to accept, rather than a surprise someone would later have to explain.

And a visible residual raises a question this chapter cannot answer: *whose is it?* A cost that has been named but whose remainder no one has agreed to carry is still an orphan — better than a hidden cost, but not yet a governed one. Someone, a named and accountable someone, has to accept the residual on the record — bounded, and revocable, and theirs. That is the modern echo of Morris pledging his own name against the shortfall: the guarantor who stands behind what the controls could not eliminate. We will build that acceptance into the architecture in Chapter 27, when we ask what it takes to govern at the full parity of a serious human institution.

For now, hold the two halves together. A cost named by construction — surfaced before approval, in its four parts, in the right order, pointed inward as well as out — is the difference between a decision and a gamble. And the residual it leaves behind is the difference between a decision that is merely informed and one that is fully owned. The named cost tells you the price. The next primitive makes sure that nobody can later pretend they were never told it — the record.

The Record

Every consequential decision in Parts I and II eventually met the same question, and the whole worth of a governed system can be measured by whether it can answer it: *why did it do that, and who approved it?*

In the failures of Part II, that question arrives too late and finds nothing. The forwarding machine passed the action along but witnessed nothing, so there is traffic but no reasoning. The safeguard had no attendant, so the alert fired into a void. The captured system stopped being audited, so there is no trail to follow. In each case the answer to "why, and who?" is a reconstruction — people in a room after the fact, assembling a plausible story from fragments, because the actual reasoning and the actual authority were never captured at the moment they existed. This chapter is about a system where that question has an answer *by construction*, because the system could not have taken the action without creating one.

Sit in the incident review that such a system makes possible, because the contrast is the whole point. Something went wrong last Tuesday — a large refund issued that should never have been. In most organizations the next two weeks are archaeology: pulling logs from four systems, interviewing whoever was on shift, reconstructing from memory and timestamps a story that is plausible and unfalsifiable in equal measure. In a governed operation the review is a lookup. The refund is a decision record. It says what was proposed and by which agent, what the named cost was and how the system sized it, who approved it and on what authority, what evidence the reasoning rested on, and whether anyone — a human, or the system's own certainty floor — dissented. The question *why did it do that, and who approved it?* is not investigated. It is *read.* Those two weeks of archaeology were never the cost of the incident; they were the cost of not having kept the record — and a governed operation does not pay it.

The decision record

When engineers make a significant architectural choice, the good ones write an Architecture Decision Record — a short, permanent note that captures what was decided, what the alternatives were, why this one won, and who made the call. Its value is not in the moment; it is years later, when someone asks why the system is shaped this way and the record answers instead of a shrug. The primitive at the center of a governed operation is the same idea, moved from design time to *run* time and made mandatory: every consequential action produces a **decision record**, automatically, as an inseparable part of taking the action.

And the record is not a log line. It carries the full anatomy of the governed decision: the **named cost** that was surfaced — the burn, the ripple, who pays, the reversibility; the **gate** that was passed — who proposed and which different party approved; the **authority** exercised — the two axes, the level the actor was cleared for and the impact the action carried; any **dissent** that was registered, the "no" kept beside the "yes" in George Read's tradition; and the **lineage** — the evidence and reasoning the decision rested on, recorded rather than relayed. All of it, captured at the instant of decision, and then made **immutable**: not editable after the fact, not quietly rewritable, so that the record of why remains what it was when it mattered rather than what someone later wished it had been. How that immutability is achieved is a matter for after the filings. What it *guarantees* is enough here: the past cannot be silently edited to fit the present.

One ledger, two actors

Now the move that makes this more than a better audit log, and it is the insight this whole architecture turns on.

A human decision and a machine decision produce the *same kind of record.* Not two systems — one for people, one for agents — but one ledger, in which the actor is simply a field. When a person approves a consequential action, it is recorded, with its cost and its authority and its dissent. When an agent proposes one and a person approves it, it is recorded in exactly the same shape. The human and the machine are not governed by parallel regimes that someone must later reconcile; they are governed by one regime that records them identically, and the gate is the point where the two meet on a single act.

Picture a single afternoon on a claims desk. At 2:14 a human adjuster approves a large settlement; at 2:15 an agent proposes another and a supervisor approves it; at 2:16 the same agent, denied by its own certainty floor on a third, records the decline. Three decisions, two kinds of actor — and in the ledger they are three entries of the *same* shape, each with its named cost, its authority, its approver, its dissent, distinguishable only by a field that says whether the proposer was a person or a model. When the regulator comes, they do not ask for the "AI log" and the "human log" and try to stitch them together; there is one log, and the machine's decisions sit in it under the same columns as the people's, held to the same account. That single-shape record is the whole reason a governed operation never grows the seam everyone else is discovering the hard way — the seam between how you govern your people and how you govern your machines.

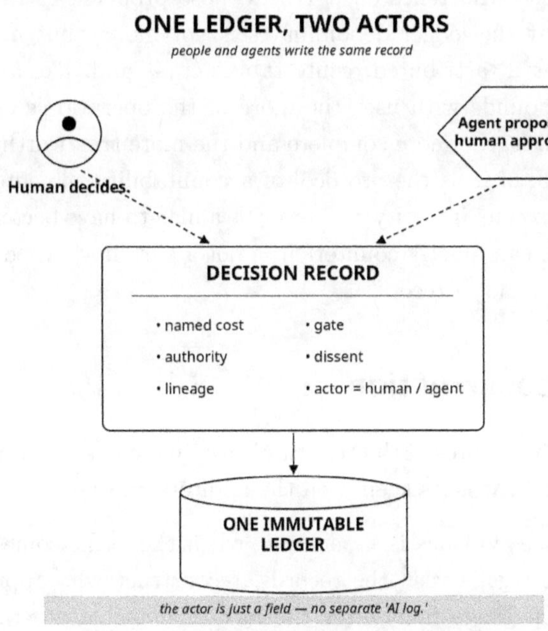

Figure 8: One ledger, two actors: people and agents write the same record — the actor is just a field.

This is what it means to say the architecture *carries the human system forward* rather than bolting a separate "AI governance" apparatus onto the side. There is no separate apparatus. There is one ledger of consequential decisions, and machines are simply new actors writing into the record that people were always supposed to keep.

That unification is worth pausing on, because it dissolves a problem everyone else is struggling with. The industry is building "AI governance" as a distinct discipline with distinct tools, sitting beside the ordinary governance of the enterprise, and then discovering that the two do not talk to each other — that the AI has a separate audit trail nobody cross-references with the human one. A governed operational system never has that seam, because it never made the split. A decision is a decision. Who or what proposed it is a property of the record, not a reason for a second system.

It is worth naming what this ledger actually is, because the ordinary words undersell it. It is not a log, and not an archive. It is closer to a *currency* — a shared medium whose entire value is its integrity. A banknote works because it cannot be counterfeited or spent twice; a governed decision record works because it cannot be forged, back-dated, or quietly rewritten, and because everyone who relies on it trusts those properties without having to check. What the ledger denominates is not money but *accountability* — a costed, gated, attributed, contestable act — and, like any currency, its worth compounds with use: the more of the operation's decisions are minted through it, the more complete and the more trustworthy the whole becomes. Think of it as the protocol of accountability the enterprise runs on, and the reason its integrity can never be a nice-to-have becomes obvious. A currency you can quietly counterfeit is not a currency. A ledger you can quietly rewrite is not a record.

Audit by construction

This is where the failures of the "capture" family are answered directly, and where the record earns its keep with the auditors and regulators.

Most compliance evidence is *assembled*: when the audit comes, teams go and gather the logs, screen the records, reconstruct who approved what, and present a package built after the fact to demonstrate that controls were followed. The trouble with assembled evidence is that it is only as honest as the assembly, and Part II is a catalogue of reasons the assembly goes wrong. A governed operation does not assemble its evidence. The evidence *is* the operation. The record exists because the system could not have acted without emitting it — the trail is a by-product of doing the work, not a separate chore performed for the assessor. This is **audit by construction**, and it inverts the entire economics of compliance: instead of proving after the fact that you probably followed the controls, you have, by construction, a complete and immutable record that you did — every consequential act, with its cost, its approver, and its reasoning, already there.

When a framework demands record-keeping over a system's lifetime, or a trustworthy audit trail — and in the final chapter we will see that every one of them does, in its own dialect — this is the answer that is *met* rather than *promised.* The log is not something the organization commits to maintain. It is something the system cannot help but produce.

The record has a family

I will end on the thread that ties Part III together and points at its climax, because you can already see it forming.

I have described *the* decision record as if there were one kind. There is not — there is a *family.* An ordinary governed action produces one shape of record. But an authorization — a named authority accepting the residual risk — is also a record, of a slightly different type. A contest, when someone appeals a decision, is a record. A delegation, when authority is lent to an agent, is a record. A release, when something crosses a boundary, is a record. Every governance act, whatever its kind, turns out to be a *typed* entry in the one immutable ledger — same DNA, different type. Hold that observation lightly for now; it is the seed of the argument in Chapter 28 that all of this is a small algebra rather than a pile of features.

There is one last thing the record forces us to confront, and it is the hardest problem in the book. An immutable ledger of every consequential decision is a magnificent thing for accountability — and a dangerous thing for any organization that has information it is legally or existentially obligated *not* to expose. The moment you can prove everything, you can be compelled to reveal everything. A record that governs the whole enterprise is worthless to a hospital, a law firm, or a defense program if keeping it means surrendering the very confidences they are sworn to protect. So the ledger that governs everything must itself be governed — and that requires a capability nothing so far in this book has provided. It is the one piece that had to be genuinely new.

The Sealing Layer

Here is the objection that kills every governance system before this one, and it is not a technical objection. It is an existential one.

Imagine trying to sell the system I have described so far — the gate, the ladder, the named cost, the immutable record of every consequential decision — to a hospital, a law firm, or a defense program. They will follow you all the way through the record chapter, nodding, and then they will stop, because you have just described a machine that captures and permanently preserves the reasoning behind every decision they make. And some of what they decide is *privileged.* Some of it is *classified.* Some of it is the exact category of information they are legally and ethically sworn never to expose. You have offered them perfect accountability at the price of perfect discoverability, and for them that is not a trade. It is a disqualification. A record that governs everything is useless to an institution that must, for the most serious reasons, keep some things unrecordable.

This is the false choice the sealing layer exists to dissolve: *govern it* or *keep it secret*, pick one. Regulated and classified institutions have been picking "keep it secret," which is why so much consequential decision-making happens in exactly the ungoverned shadows this book is trying to end. The commercial world calls the protected thing *privilege*; the defense world calls it *classification.* It is the same need in two vocabularies: the ability to hold something so that it is governed and yet never exposed.

Why access control is not enough

The naive answer is access control — encrypt the sensitive content, restrict who can read it, log the access. Every system has this, and for this problem it is not enough, for one decisive reason: if the platform can grant access, the platform can be *compelled* to grant access. A lock whose key is held by the custodian is a lock the custodian can be ordered — by a court, a subpoena, a regulator, or an adversary who compromises the custodian — to open. Ordinary confidentiality protects your data from everyone except the party holding the platform, and the party holding the platform is precisely who a legal process, or a breach, comes for. For information whose exposure is catastrophic, "we control who can see it" is not a guarantee. It is a promise that lasts exactly until someone with enough authority tells the platform to break it.

Concretely: a law firm runs its matters on a governed system, and the system faithfully records the reasoning behind every consequential decision — including the privileged analysis its lawyers would never surrender. Two years later the firm is in litigation, and opposing counsel serves a subpoena on the *platform vendor.* If the vendor can produce the plaintext — if any key in the vendor's possession opens that reasoning — then the firm's privilege is now only as strong as a vendor's willingness and ability to resist a court order, which is to say not strong at all. The firm has not gained governed accountability; it has created a new, softer target for compelled disclosure, sitting outside its own walls. That is the precise failure the rest of this chapter has to rule out — not by promising the vendor will refuse, but by making it so the vendor *cannot* comply.

The defense version is the same shape wearing a uniform. A program office runs classified decisions on the same kind of system — target development, source protection, compartmented planning — and the identical question decides whether it can adopt at all: can anyone outside the cleared chain, the vendor included, be compelled or compromised into opening what was sealed? If the platform holds a key to a compartment, the platform is now a path into that compartment that does not run through the clearance system built to guard it — a spill waiting for a subpoena, a breach, or a single bad actor with vendor access. Commercial calls the thing it must protect *privilege*; defense calls it *classification*; the mechanism that fails them is one mechanism, and the guarantee that saves them is one guarantee. That is why a single capability serves both worlds — the lawyer and the program office are asking the identical question, and it has one right answer.

The platform must be unable to open it

So the guarantee has to be stronger, and stating it plainly is the whole contribution of this chapter: the platform must be *structurally unable* to open the sealed thing. Not unwilling. Not policy-restrained. *Unable.*

That means the ability to unseal cannot rest with the platform at all. The custody of what unlocks a protected space has to live outside the platform's control, and unsealing has to require the cooperation of parties the platform cannot stand in for — a threshold of holders, no one of whom, platform included, can open it alone. This is what I mean by a **protected enclave** governed by **zero-knowledge custody**: the system can *hold* the sealed content, can prove it exists, can record that it was created and governed — while being genuinely incapable of reading it, because the means to read it were never in its hands. When a compulsion arrives at the platform, the honest and complete answer is not "we would rather not." It is "we cannot" — and that answer is true because it was built to be true, not asserted because it is convenient.

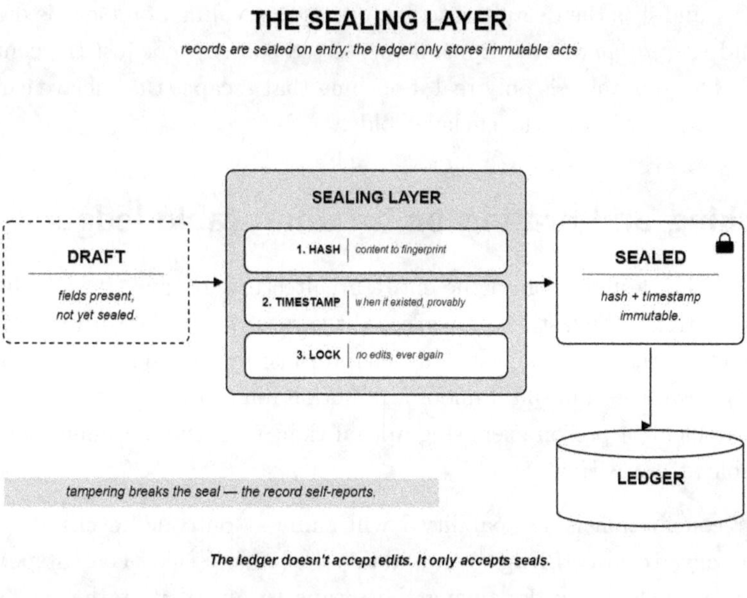

Figure 9: The sealing layer: the accountable record stays open; the protected body is sealed — governed, yet never exposed.

The commercial institution and the defense program need exactly this same guarantee, which is why one architecture serves both. The lawyer needs a place where privileged reasoning can be governed without becoming discoverable through the platform. The program needs a place where classified material can be governed without the platform becoming the leak. Same primitive, two worlds.

The false lock

There is a subtle way to get this wrong that looks completely right, and it is worth naming because it is the trap a careful engineer falls into.

You seal the sensitive source document perfectly — encrypted, enclave-held, uncompellable. And then, to make the content *useful* to the system, you let the machine read it once and keep a processed, searchable representation of what it learned — the derived index that lets an AI retrieve and reason over the material. That representation is plaintext in every way that matters: it encodes the substance of the thing you sealed, sitting outside the enclave, fully readable by the platform. You have locked the front door and left the contents photographed in the hallway. A seal that protects the original while leaking its meaning through everything derived from it is a **false lock** — and it is the default outcome unless the sealing boundary is drawn around *everything* derived from the protected content, not just the content itself. The guarantee is only real if nothing that escapes the enclave carries the substance of what the enclave holds.

Locking and erasing on an immutable ledger

Now the hardest tension in the entire architecture, because it looks like a contradiction. The last chapter insisted the record must be **immutable** — no quiet rewriting of the past. This chapter insists that some content must be *destroyable* — a hospital under a retention limit, a program sanitizing a compartment, a person exercising a legal right to erasure. Immutable and erasable at once. How?

The reconciliation is a capability I will name at outcome level and leave there: **crypto-shredding** — the ability to render sealed content permanently unreadable by destroying the means to unseal it, rather than by editing the record that holds it. The immutable ledger keeps its unbroken history — the fact that a decision was made, when, by whom, under what authority, all still there, still un-rewritten. But the *sensitive body* inside a protected enclave can be made unrecoverable on demand, cleanly, without falsifying the history that references it. You get both properties that seemed to exclude each other: the account of what happened is permanent, and the protected content within it can be honored under a retention limit, a legal hold, or a right to be forgotten. The ledger that governs everything is itself governed — including by the discipline of forgetting what it must not keep.

What this answers, and what it does not

This is also the answer to the discoverability worry that has been shadowing the book since the record chapter. Yes, an immutable record is legally discoverable — and that is mostly a feature, because a governed record is a *duty-of-care defense*: proof that you named the cost, gated the act, and can show exactly how a decision was made. The prudent posture is not to avoid keeping records; it is to keep the accountable record openly and to place only the genuinely protected residual — the privileged, the classified, the material whose exposure is catastrophic — inside the enclave, where it is governed but sealed. Most of what an organization "leaves unsaid" to avoid discovery should instead be *said and sealed.*

And I have to end on the honest limit, because a chapter that oversold this would commit the book's own cardinal sin of manufacturing certainty. Sealing makes the content uncompellable *at the platform.* It does not make it court-proof in the world. The parties who together hold the means to unseal can still, themselves, be compelled — a court can still order the human key-holders to act. What the architecture guarantees is narrower and still transformative: the platform is removed as the point of compromise and the point of compulsion. The custody returns to the humans and institutions who are supposed to hold it, under their own legal protections, rather than pooling in a vendor who can be ordered to hand it over. That is not a magic trick that puts information beyond all law. It is the difference between a confidence protected by its rightful holders and one silently surrendered by the software they happened to run on.

That is the one capability in this whole architecture that had to be genuinely new — and it is the reason a regulated or classified institution can adopt any of the rest of it.

Dissent, Restraint, and No Figurehead

The primitives so far are muscular — a gate that stops, a ladder that ranks, a cost that surfaces, a record that remembers, a seal that protects. They are all, in a sense, about *action*: making the system act only when it should, and remember that it did. This chapter is about three disciplines that are quieter, and easier to leave out, and that separate a system which merely works from one that can be trusted over years. They are the architectural forms of the human virtues Part I began with — dissent, restraint, and the refusal of a single point of authority.

The dissent that is kept

Return to George Read one last time — the man who voted no and signed anyway — because his discipline becomes, in this architecture, a specific and buildable thing.

In most systems, disagreement is transient. Someone objects, the objection is discussed, the decision is made, and the objection evaporates — it lives, at best, in someone's memory and, at worst, nowhere at all. The decision that emerges looks clean and unanimous whether or not it was. A governed system does not let the objection evaporate. When a decision is made over a registered dissent — a human who disagreed, or the system's own certainty floor declining to concur — that "no" is *kept*, permanently, in the record, beside the "yes." Not as a footnote to be sanded away, but as part of the decision's permanent anatomy.

The payoff is the one dissent always promised, now guaranteed rather than hoped for. When the decision runs into trouble later, the question "did anyone see this coming?" has an answer that is a name and a date rather than a shrug. The dissent record turns the most perceptive objection in the room — the one a captured culture teaches people to swallow — into a preserved asset that pays out at precisely the moment an organization is tempted to pretend no one knew. A system that keeps its dissent cannot manufacture false unanimity, because the disagreement is in the record, uneditable, waiting.

You can see the value in a single after-action meeting, the kind every organization eventually has. A model was approved a year ago to auto-approve a class of loans, over the recorded objection of one risk analyst who thought the training data under-represented a particular segment. She was outvoted; the decision was reasonable at the time; it shipped. This year that exact segment shows a spike in defaults. In an organization without a kept dissent, the after-action is a fog — *did anyone raise this?* — and the honest answer is a shrug, because the objection lived in a meeting a year gone and the minutes, if they exist, do not capture it. In a governed one, the dissent is in the decision's own record, with her name, the date, and the specific concern, and the meeting is short: she saw it, she said so, she was overruled, and here is exactly what she said. That record does two things at once. It vindicates the person who was right — which is how you keep such people willing to speak next time — and it tells you precisely where to look, because the objection *named the failure mode a year before it arrived.* A swallowed "no" would have cost you both.

Restraint, built in

The second discipline is restraint, and Part II taught us it fails in both directions — the guardian that never lets go, and the caution that never acts. A governed system needs restraint that is proportioned, and two architectural commitments give it that.

The first is the **certainty floor** from the epistemic chapter, now placed where it belongs: a system that will *decline.* Asked for a verdict the evidence does not support, it returns an honest "I cannot tell" rather than a manufactured answer — and, crucially, that decline is itself recorded, a dissent against its own pressure to perform. Restraint here is not silence; it is a legible refusal, on the record, to claim more than it knows.

The second is a design posture I will state as a maxim, because it is the antidote to the guardian that never steps back: *a governed system is built to be useful without being necessary.* It earns its place by helping, not by making itself impossible to remove. This is a deliberate refusal of the easiest path to importance — becoming load-bearing, indispensable, the thing the operation cannot run without. A system designed to be useful-but-removable is a system that can be allowed to *do less* when less is needed, that does not reach for work to justify itself, that does not quietly deskill the humans around it. Restraint, in the end, is the discipline of a powerful system choosing not to become the center — which turns out to be the hardest thing to build and the most important.

No figurehead

The third discipline is the deepest, and it is the one that guards the governance system against *itself.*

There is a temptation, when you build something this central, to route its authority through a single point — one privileged operator, one master key, one controlling account, one person or module that can override the rest. It feels safe. It is the opposite of safe, and Part II already named why: a single point of control is a single point of failure, a single point of capture, and — if it is a governance system — a single point that, compromised, corrupts everything it was built to protect.

So the mature architecture has **no figurehead.** Control is diffused deliberately, so that removing the apparent authority — the operator everyone assumes is in charge — does not change how the system behaves. This is the lesson of every story where the imposing figure turns out to be a small man working levers behind a curtain, or the powerful-seeming agent turns out not to be the thing in control at all: the authority was never really where it appeared to be. But — and this is the distinction that keeps diffusion from becoming its own danger — diffused control must be *legible,* not opaque. The point is not to hide where authority lives; it is to ensure that no single place holds it, *and that every exercise of it leaves a record.* A system with no figurehead is safe only because every consequential act, from anyone and anything, is gated and recorded. Diffusion without the record is just a conspiracy with no one accountable. Diffusion *with* the record is authority that cannot be seized, because there is no throne to seize and no move that goes unwitnessed.

The system must obey its own rules

Which brings the argument to its reflexive turn — the point where the governance system has to be held to the discipline it imposes on everything else.

A governance system that becomes the single indispensable center of an operation has committed the first sin in the catalogue. It *is* the N.I.C.E. failure — the institution that becomes the problem it was built to solve — only worse, because it is the institution whose entire job was to prevent exactly that. The thing that governs everything is the thing most dangerous to leave ungoverned. So the substrate must be governed by the rules it enforces on others: its own changes go through a gate, its own actions leave records, its own growing centrality is named as a cost, its own authority is diffused and legible. There is no privileged layer that sits above the discipline and administers it from outside. The ledger that governs everything is inside the set of things it governs.

This is not a paradox; it is the only stable arrangement. Any governance system with a trapdoor — a layer exempt from its own rules — has simply relocated the ungoverned risk to the trapdoor, and made it the most valuable target in the building. A system that obeys its own rules, all the way down, with no exempt center and no hidden hand, is the only kind that can be trusted with the role of governing everything else.

The mature governed system, then, has no man behind the curtain — and, because everything it does is recorded, it can *prove* it. That provable absence of a hidden hand is not a small thing. It is what lets an institution stake its operations on the system without staking them on the trustworthiness of whoever happens to hold the keys. And it sets up the final question of the architecture, the one that decides whether any serious institution can actually adopt this: does the system reproduce *every* control they rely on today — or does it quietly ask them to give some up?

Governing at Human Parity

There is a test that decides whether any of this architecture matters in practice, and it is not a technical test. It is a subtraction test: *when an institution adopts this system, does it have to give anything up?*

Because a serious institution — a bank, a hospital, a defense program, a regulated manufacturer — already governs itself. It has controls, and the controls are not decoration; they are the accumulated scar tissue of things that went wrong and were fixed. If a new system asks them to surrender even one of those controls as the price of adoption — if going governed-and-automated means losing a capability they have today — then the system has not advanced their governance. It has *degraded* it, however sophisticated it looks, and no responsible operator will accept that trade. This is the completeness principle, and it is the standard the whole architecture has to meet: **for every governance control a serious institution relies on today, there must be a primitive in the system that reproduces it.** The job is to carry the human governance system *forward* onto a machine-speed substrate — not to shrink it to whatever the software happened to implement.

I will spend this chapter on the four controls that are easiest to leave out, because they are the ones whose absence quietly disqualifies most "AI governance" tools. Each is a place where the human system already has an answer, and where the architecture has to have one too.

Someone owns the residual

Chapter 23 ended on an orphan: the **residual** risk that remains after every control has done its work, named but un-owned. The human governance world has a mature answer to that orphan, and it has a name. In the security and defense world it is the **Authority to Operate** — an accountable official who, having reviewed the residual risk, formally *accepts* it and signs their name to the acceptance. The system does not decide it is safe enough. A named human accepts what is left, on the record, and owns the consequences.

The architecture reproduces this exactly, and then does one thing the paper version cannot. Risk acceptance becomes a first-class record: a named authority accepts a specific residual, and the acceptance is **bounded** — scoped to particular conditions — **expiring** — good until a date, not forever — and **revocable.** And because agents operate continuously, the acceptance is *continuous* too: the authorization is tied to the conditions it was granted under, and when those conditions change — when the risk basis the official signed off on no longer holds — the authorization *lapses* rather than silently persisting. This is the modern form of the Morris pledge from Part I: skin in the game, a named guarantor standing behind what the controls could not eliminate — except now the pledge is scoped, dated, and automatically void when the ground it rested on shifts. Accountability for the residual is not a one-time signature. It is a living, expiring commitment.

A decision you cannot contest is not governed

The second control is the one an individual on the receiving end cares about most, and it is the direct answer to the phrase that has come to stand for everything people fear about automated decisions: *computer says no.*

A decision that cannot be contested is not a governed decision. It is a verdict, and a verdict with no appeal is not accountability — it is just power with a clean interface. Every mature governance system, and an increasing body of law, requires that a consequential decision about a person be *contestable*: that there be a way to challenge it, to demand a human review, to force the decision to justify itself to someone with the authority to overturn it. This is not a courtesy. It is what makes redress possible at all.

The architecture makes contestability real by resting it on the record. You cannot meaningfully appeal a decision whose reasoning was never captured — there is nothing to examine, nothing to challenge, only an outcome. But every consequential decision in this system carries its named cost, its authority, its lineage, its dissent. So an appeal has something to work with: the actual basis of the decision, laid out, reviewable, overturnable. And here the book's oldest thread closes. The **party not yet in the room** — the one who bears the cost of a decision they were absent for — finally gets a way in. The appeal is the door. Contestability is how the person the decision was *about* becomes, after the fact, a person the decision must *answer to.*

Make it concrete with the case people fear. Someone is denied a loan, a benefit, a job screen, by a system, and asks why. In the ungoverned version they get the sentence that has become a symbol of the age: *the computer says no* — and no one in the building can tell them more, because no one in the building knows; the reasoning was never kept. In the governed version the denial is a decision record. The appeal does not begin with archaeology; it begins with the actual basis of the decision — the factors, the named cost, the authority under which it was made, the confidence, any dissent — and a human reviewer with the power to overturn it can see exactly what the system saw and judge whether it was right. The difference is not that a governed system never denies anyone; it will. The difference is that its denials can be *answered to*, which is the whole distinction between a decision and a decree.

Borrowed authority, never orphaned

The third control answers the question every board and every general counsel asks first about autonomous agents, and rightly: *who is to blame when the AI does it?*

The architecture's answer is that an agent never has authority *of its own.* Whatever an agent is permitted to do, it does on **borrowed authority** — delegated to it by an accountable principal, and that delegation is **bounded** (limited in scope), **traceable** (you can always follow it back), **revocable** (it can be withdrawn), and **terminating in a human.** Follow any agent's authority up the chain and it must end at a named person or body who is answerable for it. There is no such thing, in a governed system, as authority that belongs to the machine itself — because authority that belongs to no one is exactly the orphan that makes "who is to blame?" unanswerable.

This is delegation as every human institution already practices it. A manager delegates to a subordinate without surrendering accountability; a principal authorizes an agent within limits; command authority flows down a chain and responsibility flows back up it. The architecture insists an artificial agent live inside that same discipline: it acts because someone accountable lent it the authority to, within limits that someone accountable set, and that someone remains answerable. **No orphan authority.** When the agent acts, the question "on whose authority?" always has a name at the end of it.

Trace it through the moment it matters — the moment after something has gone wrong. An agent cancels a large shipment, and it turns out to be a mistake that costs a customer their contract. In an ungoverned deployment the question *who authorized this?* has no clean answer: the agent did it, the agent is not a legal person, the vendor points to the customer's configuration, the customer points to the vendor's model, and accountability dissolves into the gap between them — the orphan. In a governed one, the cancellation carries its borrowed authority in the record. Follow it up: the agent acted under a delegation scoped to shipment adjustments below a threshold, granted by a named operations lead, under a policy approved by a named executive — bounded, revocable, dated. The chain terminates in people. The answer to *who is to blame?* is not "the AI" — the non-answer that has let more than one organization walk away from a harm — but a specific human who lent the authority and a specific human who set its limits, each of whom can be asked why. That is the point: autonomy did not open a new place for accountability to leak out. The authority the agent used was always someone's, and the record says whose.

A boundary is a governed event

The last control is the one that the classified world and the regulated commercial world both need, and that almost every system gets wrong by treating a boundary as a wall rather than as an event.

Information constantly needs to cross boundaries — between a company and its partner, between a program and a coalition ally, between one compartment and another. The failure mode is *spillage*: the sensitive thing crossing a boundary it should not, or crossing shorn of the restrictions that were supposed to travel with it. The human world governs this with caveats and handling instructions and clean-room agreements — rules about what may cross, to whom, under what constraints. The architecture makes a boundary crossing a **governed release**: a first-class, recorded event, in which the caveats *travel with* the content rather than being left behind at the wall. What could be shared is shared; the restrictions on it move with it; and the crossing is recorded like any other consequential act.

The same primitive serves both worlds because the need is identical under different names. In defense, it is coalition sharing — releasing to an ally exactly what may be released, no more, with the handling caveats intact. In commerce, it is the consortium and the clean room — partners collaborating on shared data without either side spilling what must stay its own. A boundary, governed properly, is not a wall that stops everything or a gap that leaks everything. It is a gate of its own, with a record.

The architecture does not shrink the human system

Stand back and count what this chapter added: a named owner for the residual, a right to contest, an unbroken chain of borrowed authority, and a governed way to cross a boundary. None of them is exotic. Every one is a control that serious human institutions have relied on for decades — the ATO, the appeal, the delegation, the caveat. The point of reproducing them is the completeness test with which this chapter opened: an institution adopting this system should find that *everything it could do before, it can still do* — and now at machine speed, with a record, across human and agent alike.

That is the whole claim of the architecture, stated at its most honest. It does not diminish the human governance system in exchange for automation. It reproduces it — carries it forward, intact, onto a substrate fast enough to keep up with machines and rigorous enough to hold them to the same account we hold ourselves. Which raises a question that has been building since the first primitive, and that the next chapter finally answers: if all of this reproduces what institutions already do, what exactly is *new* here — and why does it amount to a category of system the world has not had a name for?

Governance Is a Small Algebra — and a New Category

By now the apparatus may look large. Across the last several chapters we have added a gate that will not let one person approve their own proposal; a ladder that rates every action by how much of the world it can change; a cost that has to be spoken before anyone signs; a record that writes itself; a sealed vault the platform itself cannot open; a discipline of dissent, restraint, and no figurehead; and a set of mechanisms — borrowed authority, the right to appeal, the governed crossing of a boundary — that carry the human governance system forward for machines. That is a great many moving parts.

Here is the surprise, and it is the point of the whole book: **it is not large. It is small.**

Everything in Part III is a handful of primitives that *compose* — a grammar, not a feature list. Once you can see the grammar, you can read every governance requirement anyone has ever handed you, and write any new one, in the same few words.

The reveal

Count them. The **gate** — a decision is *proposed*, and a different human approves. The **named cost** — say what it costs, before you approve. The **autonomy ladder** and its two axes — how privileged is the actor, and how consequential the act; both must clear. The **immutable ledger** — the reasoning survives, and it cannot be quietly rewritten. The **sealing layer** — some of it can be governed without ever being exposed. The four

rituals — the practices that keep the built thing honest. And the **anti-pattern catalogue** — the named ways it goes wrong, so you can see them coming.

That is the entire vocabulary.

Everything else — accepting a risk, appealing a decision, delegating authority, releasing information across a boundary — is not a new mechanism. It is a *sentence* written in that vocabulary: the same primitives, arranged, producing one more kind of immutable, reasoned, attributable record in the one ledger. An authorization is a record. An appeal is a record. A delegation is a record. A release is a record. The governance of an entire enterprise — every consequential act, by a person or by a machine — turns out to be a small set of verbs and a family of typed sentences.

I did not set out to make it small. I found that it was. The discipline in this book arrived three times, independently — once from the history of people who pledged their lives to name a cost, once from the engineering of a system that had to be able to refuse, and once from first principles — and each time it reduced to the same few parts. When three roads meet at one clearing, the clearing is real. Governance is a small algebra.

Watch it compose once, on a single real act, and the claim stops being abstract. A support agent — a machine — determines that a customer is owed a refund larger than any it is permitted to issue on its own. Write the governance of that one moment in the grammar. The agent *proposes* the refund — the gate: it can propose anything, it changes nothing. The proposal carries its *named cost*: the amount, who bears it, whether it can be pulled back. The *ladder* checks the two axes — the agent's privilege and the act's impact — and the impact exceeds the agent's rung, so a human approver is required. The manager it routes to lacks the authority for a refund this size, so she *delegates* it upward: one record. The authority-holder approves, *accepting the residual risk*: another record. The whole exchange writes itself into the *immutable ledger* as a short chain of typed entries — a proposal, a delegation, an authorization, an approved action — each attributable, each costed, none rewritable. If the customer later disputes the outcome, the *appeal* is one more entry appended to the same chain. Nothing in that paragraph is a new mechanism. It is the gate, the cost, the ladder, and the record — four primitives — arranged into one sentence that happens to read, in plain English, as *an agent got a large refund approved by the right person, and all of it is on the books.* That is what it means to say governance is a small algebra: the hard-looking situations are not new machinery, they are new sentences in machinery you already have.

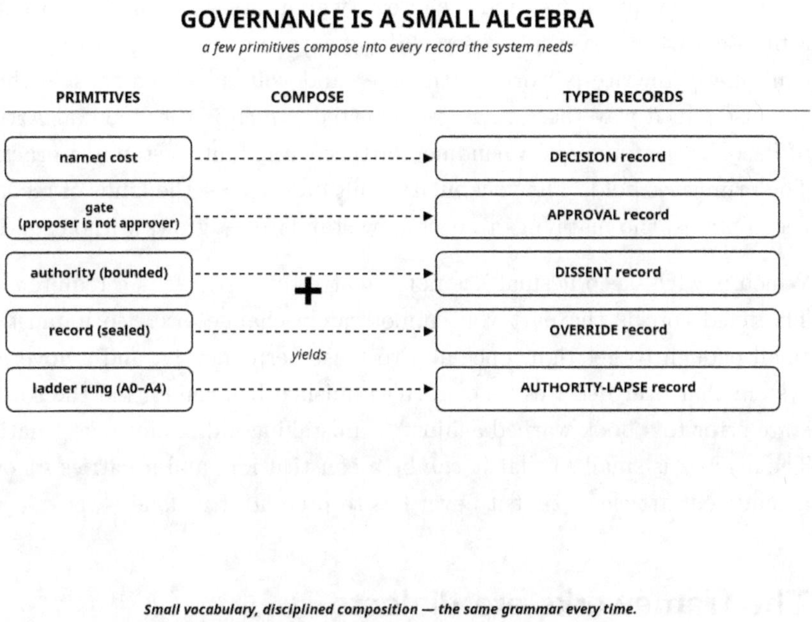

Figure 10: A small algebra: a few primitives compose into a family of typed records over one ledger.

A small algebra is a constitution

There is a reason the smallness matters beyond elegance, and it is the most practical thing in this chapter. A system meant to govern everything an organization does is, in effect, a *protocol* — a shared, trusted set of rules that every consequential act passes through — and the integrity of the record it keeps is the whole of its worth. A protocol like that faces a founding choice, and it is the same choice the framers of any durable institution face: do you let the rules accrete and evolve as you go, or do you write the essential ones down at the start, as a contract, and stand the whole thing up on them?

The founders answered it, and their answer is the one to steal. They did not write down every rule the country would ever need — they could not have, and the attempt would have frozen the republic in the assumptions of its founding. What they wrote was a *constitution*: a small set of load-bearing principles, fixed and hard to change, and — this is the part usually missed

— *the rule for how the rules change*, the amendment article, encoded in the same document. Everything else was left to evolve through that mechanism. A small algebra is exactly this kind of constitution for an operation. You encode the few primitives and the integrity guarantees at genesis — because a protocol whose base rules keep shifting earns no trust, and a ledger you can quietly rewrite is worth nothing — and you encode, alongside them, the disciplined way those rules get revisited, which is the Renewal Article of Part IV: the founders' amendment article turned into a standing practice. The primitives hold. The vocabulary built on them — the kinds of records, the domains, the mappings to each new standard — grows without end.

Which is why "keep it small" is not a matter of taste. It is a requirement. The fixed core is the part you cannot safely change later, so it must be small enough to get right once and to trust permanently; and a governed system that ever declares its own rules finished has committed the solved-state error this book warned against — mistaking a draft for a destination. The algebra is small so that it *can* be a constitution, and it carries its own amendment article so that it never has to pretend it is done.

The frameworks are dialects

This is why the standards fit — all of them, at once.

If you work in a governed industry you already carry one. SOC 2, with its segregation of duties and its change control. COSO, with its authorization and its monitoring. COBIT, with its *evaluate, direct, monitor.* The NIST AI Risk Management Framework, with *govern, map, measure, manage.* ISO/IEC 42001, the management-system standard for artificial intelligence. The European Union's AI Act — binding law now — with its *human oversight* in Article 14 and its lifetime *record-keeping* in Article 12. Six frameworks, six vocabularies, and, if you have ever had to satisfy more than one at a time, the exhausting suspicion that they are all saying the same thing in different accents.

They are. Each is a **dialect** of the grammar in this book.

"Segregation of duties," "human on the loop," "authorization control," "meaningful human oversight" — four names, in four documents, for one primitive: *proposer is not approver.* "Record-keeping," "audit trail," "traceability," "logging over the lifetime of the system" — one primitive: *the record exists by construction.* Picture the compliance officer with six binders on the shelf, each demanding, in its own tongue, that someone other than the actor sign off and that the reasons be kept. She is not managing six requirements. She is managing one, transcribed six times — and paying six times to do it.

When you can write each framework as a sentence in the same grammar, two things follow. You stop maintaining six compliance programs and start maintaining one, expressed six ways. And you see that the frameworks are *downstream*: they are dialects of a language none of them named. This book names it. The formal, assessable statement of that grammar has a name of its own — I call it the **Named Cost Framework** — but you do not need the formal version to use the idea. You need only to see that the standards on your shelf are not six problems. They are one, and it is smaller than any of them.

Substrate, not surface

There is a natural mistake to make here, and it is worth correcting before we name what we have built. You might picture governance as a layer laid *on top of* your operations — a review that happens after the work, a control bolted to the side of the system that does the real thing. It is the opposite. Governance is not on top. It is **underneath.** It is the substrate.

Think of it as a single faculty with many consumers. You build the gate, the cost, the ladder, the record, the seal *once* — and then scheduling consumes it, and finance consumes it, and the claims desk consumes it, and every agent you deploy consumes it, each inheriting the gate and the named cost and the human-approval loop for nothing. The place where your people see and sequence their work — the schedule, the board, the operational surface they touch each morning — sits *above* the substrate and draws on it. The surface is where work is arranged. The substrate is where it is governed and remembered. Confusing the two is how an organization ends up with a beautiful dashboard and no accountability underneath it.

A new category

Which brings us to the thing this book exists to name.

A system that puts that substrate *underneath everything it does* — a small governance algebra plus an immutable, typed ledger that records every consequential decision, human or agent alike, as a reasoned, costed, attributable, contestable act — is not a better version of the software you already run. It is a different kind of system. And it deserves its own name,

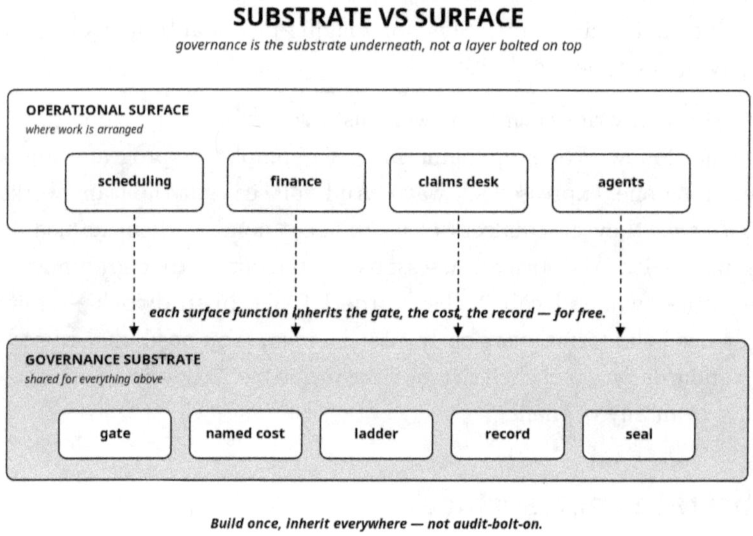

Figure 11: Governance is the substrate underneath every operational surface, not a layer bolted on top.

because you cannot ask for a thing you cannot name, and you cannot manage by a category that does not exist.

I call it a **governed operational system.**

Not "AI governance software" — that names a product you buy to watch a model from the outside. A governed operational system is the operation *itself*, run on a substrate where naming the cost, gating the act, recording the reason, and preserving the ability to contest are not features you can switch off but the ground the whole thing stands on. It spans the human and the machine by the same grammar. It spans the commercial world and the defense world by the same grammar — because, as we have seen, the grammar was never really about AI. It was about what it means for a decision to be accountable. Artificial intelligence only made the question urgent, by quietly removing the human pause that used to answer it for us.

Picture an operation actually run this way. Every consequential act — a price change, a discharge, a shipment, an agent deciding to move on its own — arrives at the same gate, carries the same named cost, and leaves the same kind of record, whether a person or a machine set it in motion. There is no separate "AI oversight" bolted to the side, because the machines and the people are governed by one grammar and write to one ledger. And when a board, a regulator, or an auditor asks the question every serious institution eventually asks — *who decided this, at what cost, and on whose authority?* — the answer is not a reconstruction assembled under pressure. It is already there, and it is a query. On a governed operational system, accountability is not something you produce when someone comes looking. It is the exhaust of ordinary operation.

Be precise about what else it is not, because the market is crowded with adjacent things it will be mistaken for. It is not a workflow engine — that routes work but never asks whether the work should happen. It is not a data warehouse or a system of record — those remember what was done but never gated whether to do it. And it is not a dashboard laid over any of them, however good the dashboard. A governed operational system sits *beneath* all of these: it is the place where the deciding happens, under discipline, before the fact. That is why it is a category and not a feature. You do not add it to your stack. You run the operation on it.

Naming it is not a flourish; it is the practical payoff of the whole argument. A category is something you can ask for, budget for, and recognize when a vendor or a team sets it in front of you — or fails to. Once *governed operational system* is a phrase you can say, "we have AI governance" stops being a sufficient answer, because you can finally see what it leaves out: a control panel bolted to the side of an operation that is, underneath, still ungoverned. Giving the thing a plain name is how you make its absence impossible to miss.

The condition

One caution, and it is the honest one. A governed operational system becomes the center of your operations only to the degree that decisions actually flow *through* it. A ledger is only as complete as what reaches it. A decision made in a hallway, in a side channel, in a spreadsheet no one governs, is invisible to the substrate no matter how good the substrate is.

So the work is not to install a recorder beside your operations and hope. The work is to make the governed surface the place where decisions are *made* — not merely where they are written down afterward. That is the difference between a system of record and a system of record-*keeping*, and it is nearly the whole difference.

What remains

On paper, the architecture is now complete. A small algebra — a few primitives, a family of typed records, one ledger — that reproduces every control a serious institution has ever relied on, for people and machines together, and carries it forward at machine speed. It is, I believe, a genuinely new category of thing, and I have tried to give it a name plain enough to build on. You do not have to build the whole of it at once — but there is now a whole of it to build, with a name and a form: a governed operational system, assembled from this fixed set of parts, that an operation can run *on* rather than merely be audited *by*.

But an architecture is inert. It guarantees only that the discipline *cannot* be skipped; it does not make anyone practice it. A gate that no one walks through governs nothing. And so the last part of this book is not more architecture. It is the practice — four rituals, each one something you can run on a Monday morning, that turn the built system into a living discipline.

The algebra is how governance becomes *possible.* The rituals are how it becomes *real.*

Part IV — The Ritual Toolkit

Part III built a system in which the discipline cannot be skipped. That is necessary, and it is not sufficient. An architecture guarantees that the gate cannot be bypassed and the record cannot be un-kept — but it does not, by itself, make anyone govern well. A gate no one thoughtfully walks through is a turnstile. The building can be perfect and the practice still absent.

So the last Part of this book is not more architecture. It is the ***practice*** *— the standing discipline that turns a built system into a governed one. Four rituals, each the human counterpart to an architectural guarantee from Part III, and each one runnable now, by hand, ahead of any software. That is deliberate. These are not features you wait for a platform to ship. They are things you can do on Monday morning with the operation you already have — which is exactly why they are also the first things a governance practice sells as a service, before a line of the platform is installed.*

Every chapter in this Part ends the same way: with an ***instrument*** *— a short, numbered procedure you can run. Read the chapter for why the ritual matters and what failure it prevents; keep the instrument as the thing you actually use. The four are the Wrongness Test, the Renewal Article, the Standing Review, and the Disconnection Drill. Together they are the standing operating discipline of a governed operation — the human practice that keeps the built system honest.*

The Wrongness Test

There is a single question that separates a governed decision from a confident one, and you can ask it out loud in any meeting, about any proposal, without a line of software: *How will you know if you are wrong?*

Watch what it does to the room. A well-governed decision has an answer ready — here are the specific things we would see if this were a mistake, here is who is watching for them, here is the point at which we stop and reconsider. A decision that is merely confident has no answer. It can tell you, at length and persuasively, why it is *right.* It cannot tell you what would make it *wrong.* And that asymmetry is the tell. A position that has marshaled every argument for itself and cannot name a single observation that would overturn it is not a conclusion. It is a belief defending itself, and Part II was a catalogue of what beliefs-defending-themselves do when they run at machine speed.

This is the first ritual, the **Wrongness Test**, and it is the human counterpart to the certainty floor from the architecture: where the system is built to decline what it cannot support, the ritual asks the humans to declare, in advance, what would prove them wrong.

Pre-registering the way you could be wrong

The discipline is simple to state and unnatural to practice: *before* a consequential decision is approved, write down the observable signals that would mean it was a mistake. Not after, when the signals are already arriving and the temptation is to explain them away. Before — while the decision is still a proposal, while you can still think clearly about it, while naming a falsifier costs you nothing but honesty.

The reason it has to be *before* is the same reason the named cost has to come before the recommendation. A falsifier invented after the fact is worthless, because a sufficiently clever system — or a sufficiently motivated person — can always explain why the bad signal does not really count, why this case is different, why the theory still holds. The only falsifier that binds is one written down before you knew how events would unfold, when you had no stake in its never firing. Pre- registration is how you tie your own hands against your future self's talent for rationalization. It is the scientist's discipline — say what result would disprove your hypothesis before you run the experiment — imported into governance, where the stakes are not a paper but an operation.

This is also the ritual that carries humility to the people who come after you. A successor who inherits a decision inherits, with it, the pre-registered falsifiers — the previous team's honest account of how this could go wrong. That is the antidote to inheriting the mechanism without the wisdom: the wisdom is written down, in the most useful possible form, as the list of things to watch for that the builders were worried about.

The most useful run of this ritual I know of produced no falsifier at all — and that was the point. A strategy team was about to commit a large budget to a new market on the strength of a forecast everyone in the room believed. Before sign-off, someone asked the question: *what would we see, in six months, that would tell us this was wrong?* The room went quiet — not because the answer was hard, but because they realized they did not have one. Every signal they could name, they could already explain away in advance; whatever happened, the thesis would survive it. That silence *was* the finding, the one the ritual exists to force: they did not have a decision, they had a conviction wearing a decision's clothes. They did not cancel the plan. They spent two more weeks until they could name three specific things that would prove them wrong — and one of the three fired four months later, and because it had been named in advance, they turned the budget off instead of doubling down to defend a forecast they had never really tested. The ritual's best day is often the one where it hands you nothing but a silence you cannot fill, and makes you notice it.

Running it

In practice the Wrongness Test lives at the gate, attached to consequential decisions — the ones high enough on the ladder to deserve the ceremony. When a decision is proposed, its falsifiers are registered alongside it: specific, measurable, dated signals, each with someone assigned to watch for it and a threshold that trips a review. Then the decision proceeds, and the falsifiers wait in the record.

The whole ritual earns its keep at the moment a falsifier fires. Because here is what happens without it: a decision starts going wrong, the signals accumulate, and each one is individually explained away, because no one ever committed in advance to what the signals would mean. The decision continues, silently, past the point where it should have been stopped — the certainty too old to hear its own doubt. With the ritual, a fired falsifier is not a matter for interpretation. It was pre-registered as the thing that means "we were wrong," and its firing forces a review rather than a rationalization. The decision does not get to quietly continue. It has to be re-decided, in the open, by people looking at the signal they told themselves to watch for.

That is the payoff, and it is worth the small discomfort of the ritual: a decision that is wrong gets *caught*, on the schedule its own authors set, instead of drifting until it becomes an incident.

The moment it works is quiet and unglamorous, which is the point. A team approving an aggressive change to a pricing model is asked, before sign-off, to name what would tell them it had gone wrong. After some grumbling they write three signals — one of them a specific rise in a particular segment's cancellation rate, checked weekly, tripping a review at a stated threshold. The change ships and the top-line numbers are good — good enough that, in a team without the ritual, the story would end there. Six weeks later the cancellation signal trips. It is small, and it would have been easy to attribute to a dozen other things: a seasonal blip, a competitor's promotion, noise. But the team had, in a cooler moment, already agreed that this exact signal would mean *we were wrong* — so it does not get explained away. It forces a review; the review finds a real segment the model had mispriced; the change is corrected before it becomes the kind of number that turns up in a board deck under a bad headline. Nobody was a hero. The ritual just made it impossible not to look.

The instrument

Run this for any consequential decision — anything high enough on the autonomy ladder to be gated. It needs no software; it needs a decision, a record, and someone willing to ask the question.

1. **State the decision and its named cost.** Write down what is being approved and what it costs — what it burns, the ripple, who pays, whether it can be undone.
2. **Pre-register the falsifiers.** *Before* approval, write the observable signals that would mean "we were wrong." Make each one specific, measurable, and dated. If you cannot name one, that is itself the finding — you have a belief, not a decision.
3. **Set the check.** Name who watches for those signals, how often they look, and what threshold trips a review.
4. **Bind it to the record.** Keep the falsifiers with the approval, so a later reviewer can see exactly what the deciders committed to being wrong about.
5. **On a trip, stop and re-decide.** A fired falsifier forces a review — an item for the Standing Review of Chapter 33 — never a silent continuation.

The tell of a system, or a person, that fails this test: they can explain at length why they are right, and cannot say what would make them wrong.

The Wrongness Test keeps a single decision honest at the moment it is made. But decisions do not stay made — the world they were right for drifts out from under them, and a decision no one ever revisits becomes a rule everyone follows and no one believes. Guarding against *that* is the next ritual.

The Renewal Article

Every organization is carrying rules that everyone still follows and no one still believes.

You know the ones. The threshold that was set for a reason nobody present can quite reconstruct. The policy that made sense for a business that no longer exists. The configuration that was correct on the day it was chosen and has been quietly wrong for two years, obeyed out of habit and the vague sense that someone must have had a reason. These are not failures of intelligence or diligence. They are the natural sediment of any operation that makes decisions and then moves on — decisions calcify into facts, facts into assumptions, assumptions into the invisible furniture of how things are done. And the furniture is never re-examined, because re-examining it is nobody's job and questioning it feels faintly absurd. It has been true for so long.

This is the failure the architecture chapters called the solved state and the certainty too old to hear its own doubt, arriving not as a dramatic error but as slow drift. The second ritual, the **Renewal Article**, is the discipline that catches it — a scheduled forcing of the question the furniture never gets asked: *is this still true?*

The living generation revisits the rules

The founders, characteristically, saw this coming. One of them held a conviction that unsettled his peers and still unsettles us: that no generation has the right to bind the next forever, that the living generation should periodically revisit the rules it inherited and re-earn or revise them rather than obey them out of mere inheritance. Founding language, on this view, should be written so that it can *challenge* your successors as much as your enemies — so that those who come after are handed not just the rules but the standing to question them. Call it the Jefferson Principle[1]. It is the opposite of the way most institutions treat their own foundations, as sacred and settled, and it is exactly the discipline a governed operation needs, because a rule that cannot be revisited is a certainty with no way to hear its own doubt.

The Renewal Article turns that conviction into a calendar item. It takes the standing assumptions a system runs on — its rules, its thresholds, its configurations — and it *resurfaces* them, on a schedule, and forces an explicit answer to whether each is still true. Not a silent renewal by default. An active re-affirmation or a revision, signed, on the record.

There is a particular human moment this ritual creates, and it is worth naming because it is where the value lives. A compliance team ran its annual renewal over a policy that had governed how the firm handled a certain kind of customer complaint for eleven years. *Still true?* Around the table, heads began to nod on reflex — and then the newest member, who had spent a year quietly enforcing the thing, said what no one else had: *"I don't think any of us actually believes this anymore. We follow it because it's the policy, and it's the policy because we follow it."* The room recognized it instantly, the way you recognize a fact you have been avoiding. The policy had not been wrong when it was written; the firm, its customers, and the law had all moved, and the rule had simply outlived the beliefs that authored it, still obeyed out of momentum. Without the renewal, that sentence never gets said, because nothing ever *asks* — and everyone keeps following a rule no one believes, which is one of the quietest and most common ways an institution loses its integrity: not by breaking its rules, but by keeping ones it has stopped meaning.

The silent pass is the enemy

The single most important feature of this ritual is what it forbids: the silent pass. In an ordinary review, the default is continuation — if no one raises an objection, the rule persists, unexamined, for another cycle. That default is precisely the mechanism by which stale certainties survive: they are never affirmed, they are simply never challenged, and the absence of challenge is mistaken for continued validity.

The Renewal Article inverts the default. For each standing assumption, someone must *actively* answer "still true?" — and a non-answer is not permitted to count as yes. Either a named person re-affirms the rule, putting their signature on the claim that it still holds, or someone writes the revision. The point is not to change everything on a schedule; most rules, re-examined, will be re-affirmed, and that is a fine outcome — a re-affirmed rule is a living commitment rather than dead furniture. The point is that the re-affirmation has to be *made*, by someone willing to own it now, in current conditions, rather than inherited by default from people who chose it under conditions that may no longer exist.

And when a rule *is* revised, the ritual insists on one more thing: mark the gap. Record what was believed then and what is believed now, so the change is legible — a versioned history of the organization's own thinking, not a silent overwrite that erases the fact that anyone ever thought differently. This is the dissent record's cousin: just as a governed decision keeps its "no" beside its "yes," a governed rule keeps its old form beside its new one, so that the evolution of the institution's beliefs is itself part of the record.

Running it

The cadence follows the stakes. Live operational controls — the thresholds and rules that govern day-to-day consequential action — deserve a frequent rhythm, quarterly or so, because the world they respond to moves quickly. Founding policy — the deep commitments, the values, the rarely-touched constitution of how the organization governs itself — can be revisited on a longer horizon, but it must still be revisited; the things we examine least are exactly the things most likely to have gone stale unnoticed.

Crucially, a revision that comes out of a Renewal Article is not a quiet edit. A changed rule is a *proposal* — it goes through the gate, like any other consequential change, with its cost named and a second party approving. The ritual surfaces the need for change; the architecture governs the change itself. Renewal without the gate would just be a new way to make unreviewed edits. Renewal *through* the gate is how an organization updates its own rules with the same discipline it applies to everything else.

You feel the value the first time a renewal turns up a rule no one can defend. A risk team sits down to its quarterly re-affirmation and reaches a threshold that has governed a whole class of transactions for years. *Still true?* The person who owns it opens his mouth to say yes — and stops, because he realizes he does not actually know why it is set where it is. He inherited it; so did the person before him. They track it down: it was calibrated for a product line the company exited three years ago, and it has been quietly mis-serving every product since — too cautious here, too loose there — obeyed the whole time out of nothing but momentum. The rule was not wrong when it was written. It simply outlived the world it was written for, and no one had ever been *required* to ask. The renewal required it, and the silent pass — the default *leave it, it's always been fine* — was the one move the ritual would not allow.

The instrument

Run this on a schedule against the standing assumptions your operation depends on. It needs a calendar, a list, and someone willing to sign.

1. **Inventory the standing assumptions.** List the rules, thresholds, and configurations a system currently runs on — and, for each, the rationale it was originally set with.
2. **Set the cadence.** Quarterly for live controls; annually (or longer) for founding policy. Put it on the calendar as an obligation, not an aspiration.
3. **Re-affirm or revise, explicitly.** For each item, answer *still true?* A silent pass is not allowed: someone signs the re-affirmation, or someone writes the revision.
4. **Mark the gap.** Record what was believed then versus what is believed now, so the *change* is legible — a versioned history, never a silent overwrite.
5. **Route revisions through the gate.** A changed rule is a proposal, not a quiet edit — cost named, second party approving, recorded like any consequential decision.

The Wrongness Test keeps a decision honest at the moment it is made; the Renewal Article keeps it honest as the world moves. Both, though, still assume the system's *discretion* — the scope of what it decides on its own — has stayed where it was authorized. The next ritual checks that assumption, because it is the one that quietly fails first.

The Standing Review

The most dangerous system in your operation is the one that has been right for so long that reviewing it feels like an insult. Chapter 13 called this capture-by-competence, and named the trap: excellence buys a system out of scrutiny, and the moment it is no longer scrutinized is the moment its next failure will go uncaught. The Wrongness Test and the Renewal Article keep individual decisions and rules honest. Neither of them watches the thing that fails most quietly of all: the slow, unvoted expansion of what a trusted system decides *on its own.*

That expansion is called discretion, and it creeps. A system authorized to decide a narrow class of cases handles them well, so the class is widened, informally, because it is good at it. Then widened again. Each widening is reasonable and none is ever formally approved, and one day the system is exercising far more discretion than anyone authorized — not through a seizure of power but through a thousand small, competent, unreviewed extensions. The third ritual, the **Standing Review**, exists to catch exactly this: a standing body whose job is to audit the system's accreted discretion and re-anchor it to what was actually authorized.

A review the system consents to

There is a feature of this ritual that sounds strange until you see why it is essential: the system being reviewed **consents** to the review, explicitly, and the consent is recorded.

Why does consent matter for an audit? Because resistance to review is itself the first symptom of the disease. A captured system — or a captured team, or a captured executive — signals its capture by treating scrutiny as an affront, by finding reasons the audit is unnecessary, by making the reviewer feel like the problem. So the Standing Review builds consent in as a probe. The system and its owners affirmatively agree to be audited — "yes, I consent" — and that agreement is logged. If the consent is freely given, good. If it is resisted, that resistance is not an obstacle to the review; it is the review's first and most important finding. A thing that does not want to be audited has just told you the most important thing about itself.

This is the structural answer to the guardian that never steps back. A system genuinely willing to submit its discretion to an outside body, on a standing basis, cannot easily become the unaccountable center, because it has consented, in advance and on the record, to be told to step back.

The outsider in the room

A review is only as good as its independence, and the specific way governance reviews go bad is *elder-capture*: the review board becomes staffed entirely by experts so close to the system that they share its blind spots. Everyone on the panel understands the system deeply, and precisely because they understand it deeply, they have absorbed its assumptions, and the review becomes the system nodding at itself in a mirror.

The guard is to seat, deliberately, a member who is *affected by the system but not expert in it* — a person who has to live with the consequences of the decisions but does not share the builders' worldview. Think of it as keeping the youngest, least-captured adult in the room: the one who can ask the naive question the experts have trained themselves not to ask, who has standing to say "I don't understand why this is allowed" without embarrassment, and whose stake is real because they bear the outcomes. Their non-expertise is the point. They are the part of the review that the system has not yet learned to anticipate and satisfy.

What comes to the seat, and what it leaves behind

The Standing Review needs a worklist, or it becomes a ceremony. The things that belong in front of it are the signals of drift and accreted discretion: any expansion of what the system decides on its own, the fired falsifiers from the Wrongness Tests, the incidents, the warnings that were filed and never acted on, the slow migrations up the autonomy ladder. Its central question is not "are the outputs good?" — outputs are easy to check and easy to fake confidence about. Its question is "has the system quietly widened what it decides without approval?" — and where it has, the review's job is to re-anchor it to its authorized rung.

And like every governed act in this book, the review produces a *record* — findings, decisions, and the dissents kept beside them. A reviewer who disagreed is not erased when the board moves on; the "no" is kept beside the "yes," so that a later review can see who saw what. The Standing Review is not a meeting that dissolves when it ends. It is a memory that accumulates.

One practical note, because it matters for how this book gets used: of the four rituals, this is the one most naturally run by an outside party. A standing review seat is exactly the kind of thing an organization brings in a fractional governance officer to hold — an independent, recurring authority to audit discretion, precisely because independence is the thing an internal team cannot supply for itself. The ritual and the service are the same artifact.

The consent step sounds like paperwork until the first time it isn't. A data team stood up a standing review over a fraud model everyone trusted, and the review asked, as it must, for the team's explicit consent to audit the model's accreted discretion. The team's lead — a good engineer, not a villain — found reasons to defer. The model was mid-retraining; the timing was bad; the reviewers lacked the context; surely the quarterly metrics were enough. None of it was unreasonable, and all of it, taken together, was the finding. A model that has earned its trust honestly has owners who are, if anything, *eager* to have it checked, because they believe it will pass. Owners who negotiate the terms of the audit down toward nothing are telling you something they cannot say out loud — and the standing review's most important record that quarter was not about the model at all. It read: *consent resisted; escalated.* The audit of the discretion could wait a week. The audit of the resistance could not.

The first time you run one of these, the most valuable moment usually comes from the person who understands the system least. A standing review of an automated eligibility system seats a community representative — no technical background, just someone whose neighbors live with the outcomes — at the table beside the engineers and the risk officers. Halfway through, as the experts nod along to a description of how a certain edge case is handled, she asks why the system is allowed to make that call at all without a person seeing it. The engineers have a fluent answer; they always do. But said out loud, to someone who is not already convinced, it does not survive contact — and the room realizes that a category of decision everyone had assumed was reviewed had quietly gone automatic two years earlier. No expert had flagged it, because to every expert it was simply how the system worked. It took the least-captured adult in the room to notice that the machine had wandered somewhere no one had authorized it to go.

The instrument

Stand this up as a recurring body with real authority over the system's discretion. It needs a seat, a worklist, and a record.

1. **Stand up the board.** Establish a recurring seat with authority to review the system's discretion. Include an *affected-but-not-expert* member to guard against elder-capture.
2. **Record consent.** The system and its owners explicitly consent to the audit, and the consent is logged. Resistance to review is itself a finding.
3. **Define the worklist.** Decide what comes to the seat: expanded autonomy, fired Wrongness-Test falsifiers, incidents, drift, warnings filed but never acted on.
4. **Audit the discretion, not just the outputs.** Ask whether the system has quietly widened what it decides without approval — and if it has, re-anchor it to its authorized autonomy rung.
5. **Produce a record.** Keep the findings, decisions, and dissents — a "no" kept beside a later "yes."

Three rituals now keep the system honest while it runs. The last one asks the hardest question of all, the one an organization avoids until an outage forces it: *could we still operate if this system were gone?*

The Disconnection Drill

Most organizations learn how dependent they are on a system at the worst possible moment: when it goes down. The outage hits, and in the scramble that follows they discover — not as a theory but as a crisis — that there is no longer a manual path, no one who remembers the old way, no capacity to run the operation without the thing that just failed. The dependence was total, and it was invisible, right up until it was catastrophic. Nobody chose it. It accreted, one convenience at a time, exactly as Chapter 12 described — the institution that became load-bearing while everyone was looking at something else. *Nobody voted on it becoming load-bearing.*

The fourth and final ritual, the **Disconnection Drill**, refuses to let that discovery wait for the outage. It is the discipline of periodically, deliberately, turning the system off — under controlled conditions, on your own schedule — to find out, while it is still cheap to find out, whether the operation can survive without it.

Function without you

The historical root of this ritual is the most poignant in the founders' story. Among the signers were men who did not live to see the thing they built take shape — one of them died in a duel barely a year after signing, one of the first of the fifty-six to go[12]. The lesson their early deaths pressed on the founding was unavoidable: the institution had to be built to *function without any particular person in it.* No single figure could be allowed to become the point on which the whole thing depended, because people are mortal and the republic was meant to outlast them all. Build to function without you; make the implicit explicit; leave no single point of personal failure. Call it the Gwinnett Principle.

A governed system has to meet the same standard, and the Disconnection Drill is how it proves it does. The architecture chapters set the design goal — a system *useful without being necessary*, one that earns its place by helping rather than by making itself impossible to remove. But a design goal is a claim, and a claim about indispensability is exactly the kind that quietly turns out to be false. The only way to know whether a system is truly useful-but-removable is to remove it and watch. Everything else is an assumption, and this book is against governing on assumptions.

Rehearsal, not punishment

The drill is a rehearsal, and the framing matters, because done wrong it reads as sabotage. You are not trying to break the operation or catch anyone out. You are running a fire drill — a deliberate, announced, bounded exercise whose purpose is to *observe*. Scope it tightly: one system, a defined set of decisions, a bounded window, and start small. Minutes before hours; one function before the whole operation. Announce it, so people know it is a rehearsal and not a real failure. Then remove the system for the window, and watch what happens.

Some organizations get the answer before the window even opens. A logistics company scheduled its first drill for a quiet Sunday and spent two weeks preparing to take its routing system offline for four hours — and in those two weeks the drill did its whole work without ever running, because the preparation kept surfacing reasons it *couldn't* be done. This dependency, then that one, then a third nobody had documented: a downstream partner whose systems polled theirs every ninety seconds and would alarm; a compliance report due Monday that only the system could generate; a night crew who had never once worked without it and did not know how. By the time they had listed everything that made a four-hour disconnection unsafe, they were staring at the exact map of their own over-dependence — the thing the drill exists to produce — and they had not yet switched anything off. The head of operations said the quiet part in the planning meeting: *"We built something we can't turn off, and we never decided to."* That sentence is the drill's entire payoff, and they reached it before the Sunday ever came.

What you are watching for is survival on the operation's own momentum. Did the work keep moving? What slowed down? What broke outright?

And most revealing of all: what turned out to depend on the system in ways nobody had realized — the silent couplings, the steps that everyone assumed a human still did that the system had quietly taken over? A drill surfaces those hidden dependencies in an afternoon, at no cost but a little inconvenience, instead of surfacing them in an incident at the cost of the operation.

Name the dependence as a cost

Here is where the last ritual closes the circle the whole book has been drawing, and returns to its very first page.

Whatever the drill reveals the operation cannot do without the system becomes a **named cost.** Not a vague unease about "over-reliance," but a specific, measured, written line item: *this is what this tool costs us in dependence — here is precisely what we could not do without it, for how long, at what risk.* That is the transformation this book has argued for from the beginning, applied now to the most slippery cost of all. Dependence is the classic unnamed cost — the one that is invisible until the bad afternoon, deferred with interest to whoever is on shift when the system fails. It is, in the vocabulary of the first chapter, the purest **second cost** there is: the system's help was the first cost — visible, adopted on purpose, the reason it is here at all; the dependence is the second cost that accrued quietly underneath, unnamed precisely because every day the system worked was a day the dependence looked free. A town widens its roads to fit the fire truck and inherits a maintenance bill it never priced; an operation widens itself around a system and inherits a dependence it never priced. Same shape, one turn of the screw higher — and the drill is how you finally read that second cost aloud. The Disconnection Drill drags it into the light and names it, while it is still cheap to name, and hands it to the Standing Review so that a body with authority can decide, deliberately and on the record, how much of it the organization is willing to carry.

An unnamed cost, made named. That is the whole practice, and it is fitting that the last ritual is the one that names the cost of the governance system's own success — because a system that has made itself indispensable has committed the first failure in the catalogue, and the drill is how you catch it before it is irreversible.

The first drill an organization runs almost always embarrasses it, gently, which is exactly what you want. A team confident that its operation could ride out the loss of a scheduling system for an afternoon turns it off, by arrangement, on a slow Wednesday. Within an hour they find three things they did not know. A downstream report nobody had thought about silently depended on the system's output, and now shows nothing. A junior coordinator, it turns out, had been the only person who knew the manual workaround — and she left in the spring. And the "manual fallback" everyone assumed existed was a document last updated for a process two reorganizations ago. None of it is a disaster, because it is a rehearsal — that is the entire point. Each of those three discoveries would have been a small catastrophe on the real bad afternoon, found under pressure instead of over coffee. The drill converted three future incidents into three items on a list, at the cost of one mildly awkward Wednesday.

The instrument

Run this periodically against any system your operation has come to rely on. It needs a scope, a window, and the willingness to look at what you find.

1. **Scope the drill.** Choose which system, which decisions, and a bounded window. Start small — minutes, then hours.
2. **Announce the withdrawal.** This is a rehearsal, not an outage. The point is to observe, not to punish.
3. **Remove the system.** It stops acting and advising for the window.
4. **Measure survival.** Did the operator keep running on its own momentum? What broke, what slowed, what silently depended on the system?
5. **Name the dependence as a cost.** Whatever could not run becomes an explicit, reviewed line item — *this is what the tool costs us in dependence* — and goes to the Standing Review.

The tell: a system that cannot be turned off for a rehearsal has already become load-bearing. The drill is how you learn that on a Tuesday of your choosing, rather than on the worst day of the year.

Four rituals now: a way to catch a decision that is wrong, a rule that has gone stale, a discretion that has quietly widened, and a dependence that has quietly deepened. Run together, on a standing basis, they are the human practice that keeps the built system honest. What remains is to see how they compose into a single discipline — and to close the account this book opened.

Part V — The Practice Under Pressure

Four Parts have made a claim: that a decision is not governed until its cost is named, that the discipline can be enforced by architecture rather than left to vigilance, and that the whole of it reduces to a small, composable grammar. A claim of that size has earned the right to be tested — hard, and in the open.

So this Part does not add to the architecture or the toolkit. It puts the practice under pressure. It begins with the objections — the fair, difficult questions a senior reader should be asking by now — and answers them before the close, so the call to action lands on cleared ground. Then it does the thing an honest argument must: it takes the grammar to cases where getting it wrong would matter most. A routine distribution decision, where the stakes are ordinary. A discharge in a hospital, where a life is in the balance. An autonomous use of force at machine speed, the hardest single decision a person may ever delegate. And a decision that crosses the border between sovereign nations, the widest boundary the practice will ever have to span.

Watch, through all of it, for one thing: whether each case needs some new machinery, or whether it is the same gate, the same named cost, the same record, and the same right to contest — composed for a harder problem. If the grammar holds here, it holds anywhere. That is the whole point of insisting it be an algebra and not a pile of special cases, and this Part is where the insistence is paid for.

The Objections

If you have read this far and felt no resistance, one of us has not been paying attention. The case I have made asks you to put a brake on systems you were promised would make you faster, to build discipline into software that mostly seems to be working fine, and to spend real money and political capital doing it. A serious person has objections to that. I would rather answer the strong ones, in your own words, than pretend they are not there — because the call in the next chapter only means something if it is made on cleared ground.

So here are the objections I hear most from the people best qualified to raise them, and my honest answers.

"This will slow us down — and speed is the whole point."

It is the first thing every operator says, and it deserves the first answer, because it rests on a confusion the whole book has been trying to clear. Governance does not slow down everything. The gate holds *consequential, hard-to-reverse* actions — and lets reading, analyzing, drafting, and recommending run at full speed, ungoverned, because they change nothing. Most of what a fast system does is exactly that kind of free action, and it stays free. What gets a brake is the narrow band of acts that can spend money, touch a customer, or alter a record that cannot be put back.

And on those, "slow" is the wrong axis. A system with no brake is not fast; it is merely early to the crash. The insurer in Chapter 11 cleared claims in seconds right up until the afternoon the pattern of wrong denials surfaced as a class action, and then it was slower than any competitor for two years.

Speed without a brake is not a speed advantage. It is deferred latency — velocity now, paid back with interest and a multiplier the first time the confident answer is wrong at scale. The governed operation is the one that can actually keep the speed, because it is the one that does not have to stop the whole line when the model has a bad day.

"We already have governance. We have GRC, we have SOC 2, we have a risk committee."

You do, and it is real, and it governs the wrong actor. Every one of those instruments — the audit, the risk committee, the quarterly attestation — was built for a world of *human* decision-makers acting at human speed, sampled after the fact. They assume a person in the loop who can be trained, reminded, and held accountable at the pace a committee meets. None of that reaches a model that proposes and acts a thousand times an hour, between meetings, in a channel no auditor sampled.

That is the seam the industry is discovering the hard way: the AI ends up with its own shadow trail that no one cross-references with the human one, and the existing governance simply does not see it. The frameworks you already run are not wrong — Chapter 28 showed they are dialects of the same grammar this book builds. But you hold the *policy* and not the *enforcement.* "Get a second approval" is a rule a fast system routes around without ever technically breaking it. A gate built so that a second approval is the only way the action can occur is not a rule; it is the shape of the system. What is new here is not the objective. It is that the objective becomes structural, and it covers the actor your current governance was never built to watch.

"This is over-engineering. You will bury us in process."

I share the fear, and I built the book to answer it — because a governed system that spends all its energy watching itself commits one of the eighteen failures in its own catalogue, the observer distortion, and I have no interest in prescribing it. So look at what the practice actually is. It is not a binder. It is a *small algebra* — a handful of primitives that compose — and four rituals you can run by hand on a Monday morning with no software, no budget, and no one's permission. You just read them. If this were a heavyweight compliance regime I would not have been able to write the whole practical toolkit as four short exercises.

The deeper answer is that the architecture exists precisely to let you do *less*, not more. The reason process metastasizes in most organizations is that discipline lives in human vigilance, so you pile on reviews and sign-offs and checklists trying to make fallible people be careful. Move the discipline into the structure — a gate that cannot be skipped, a record that writes itself — and you need *less* ceremony, not more, because the thing is enforced by construction rather than by everyone remembering to be diligent. Good governance feels like less friction, not more, because the friction it removes — the incidents, the archaeology, the reconstructions — is larger than the friction it adds.

"AI governance is hype. It is regulatory theater, and it will blow over."

Some of it is hype; the market always overshoots. But strip the word "AI" out of the argument and nothing in this book weakens, which is the tell that it was never really riding the hype cycle. Chapter 28 said it plainly: the grammar was never about artificial intelligence. It was about what it means for a decision to be accountable — a question older than computing, answered by people who pledged their lives to it in 1776. Artificial intelligence did not create the question. It only made it urgent, by removing the human pause that used to answer it for us.

And two things are not theater. The failures in Part II are not forecasts; they are the shapes of things already happening in operations like yours. And the law is not waiting for the hype to settle: the EU AI Act is binding now, with human-oversight and record-keeping obligations that read like the gate and the record described in plain regulatory language. You can bet against the hype. Betting against accountability itself is a different and worse wager.

"Our model is not good enough to trust with this." Or: "Our model is good enough that we don't need it."

I hear both, from different rooms, and they make the same mistake: they think governance is a statement about how good the model is. It is not. It is a statement about *authority*, which Chapters 21 and 22 showed is a different axis entirely from capability.

If your model is not yet trustworthy, the gate is how you deploy it safely anyway — let it propose freely, let a human hold the authority, capture the value of its intelligence without betting the operation on its judgment. And if your model is genuinely excellent, you need the discipline *more*, not less, because a better model is a more confident and more scalable way to be wrong. The brilliant system that has earned everyone's trust is exactly the one whose single subtle error gets applied ten thousand times before anyone thinks to question it. Capability raises the stakes of ungoverned authority; it never retires the need for it.

"We cannot afford to build this."

Then do not build it yet. Almost everything in this book that matters can begin with no capital at all — the ledger you started in Chapter 1, the four rituals, the exposure-gap measurement, all of which run on the operation you already have. "Start with the assessment" is the whole advice, and the assessment is a number, not a construction project.

But price the other side of the ledger honestly, the way this whole book has asked you to. The cost of *not* doing it is the classic unnamed second cost — invisible on today's budget, deferred to whoever is on shift the afternoon the ungoverned system fails, and paid then with the interest and the multiplier. "We cannot afford it" almost always means "we have not yet named what the alternative costs." Name it, in the four parts, and the arithmetic usually turns over.

"This implies we don't trust our people."

It implies the opposite — as George Read's story already showed us. A serious commitment deserves a second name on it, and the man who dissented and signed anyway was the most valuable person in the room, not the least. The gate is not surveillance and it is not a vote of no confidence. It is the structural form of the second signature a serious institution has always wanted, and the recorded dissent that a healthy one has always protected. It defends your best people, too: the proposer who did honest work is safer, not more exposed, when the record shows exactly what they proposed, what it was going to cost, and who approved it. A culture that reads a kept "no" as disloyalty is the one that does not trust its people. This is how you build the kind that does.

The objection that is the reason

Notice that the strongest objection — *this will slow us down* — is, turned over, the exact reason to do it. The pause it asks for is not friction added to a healthy system. It is the pause governance has always lived in, the one an autonomous system is specifically designed to remove, restored on purpose and only where it counts. You are not being asked to give up speed. You are being asked to keep the one brake that lets you use the speed you have without eventually wrapping the operation around a tree.

Every objection in this chapter, followed honestly to the end, arrives at the same place: not a reason the practice is unnecessary, but a more precise account of what it is for. And the best answer to the ones that remain is not more argument — it is to watch the discipline actually work, across cases of rising stakes, from an ordinary business decision to the hardest decision there is.

A Worked Assessment

I have described the assessment enough times that it is only fair to show you one. What follows is a composite — the shape of a diagnosis I have watched play out in more than one operation, with the particulars blurred — but the structure is exactly the structure, and the surprises are the surprises that actually recur. If you run anything at scale, some of this will be uncomfortably familiar.

The company is a mid-market distributor: a few hundred million in revenue, a warehouse network, a catalog in the tens of thousands of SKUs, and — like everyone now — a growing bench of automated systems making decisions that used to take a person. The leadership brought me in with a reasonable worry and a wrong question. The worry: *we are deploying AI faster than we understand it.* The wrong question: *is our AI safe?* Safe is not a measurable thing. The exposure gap is. So we did not debate safety. We measured the distance, system by system, between the level each one is *operating* at and the level its controls were actually *built* for.

Inventory the consequential decisions

The first move is not technical. It is a walk through the operation asking one question at every station: *where does a system now decide or act on something consequential with little or no human in the loop?* Not where is there AI — there is AI everywhere, most of it harmless. Where does a machine touch something that costs money, reaches a customer, or cannot easily be undone? In an afternoon we had four that mattered.

- A **replenishment agent** that forecasts demand and proposes purchase orders to suppliers.

- A **dynamic pricing engine** that sets and updates customer-facing prices across the catalog.
- A **customer-service model** that answers inbound questions about orders, returns, and accounts.
- An **accounts-payable agent** that matches invoices to receipts and releases supplier payments.

Four systems, four places the operation had quietly handed judgment to software. Now we placed each one on the ladder, twice — once for where it actually operates, once for where its controls were built to hold — and looked at the gap.

Measure each gap

The replenishment agent was deployed, eighteen months earlier, as a *suggestion* tool: it drafted proposed orders, a planner reviewed them, the planner sent them. Its controls — the light review, the planner's sign-off — were built for exactly that: a drafting assistant. But to hit a service-level target during a busy quarter, someone had switched on auto-release for any proposed order under a dollar threshold, "to save the planners time." It had never been switched back. The agent was now *authoring* purchase orders — committing the company's money to suppliers, an external and largely irreversible act — with no human in the loop for the majority of orders by count. Operating level: external, committing authoring. Control level: internal draft. The gap was two full rungs, and it was carrying real money out the door on the agent's unreviewed word every day.

The dynamic pricing engine was the one the CIO was most proud of, and it had a real gap too. It set customer-facing prices — external, visible, affecting every buyer — and adjusted them continuously with no human reviewing individual changes. Its guardrails were floors and ceilings: prices could not move outside a band. That is a genuine control, and it caught the catastrophic errors. But within the band the engine authored freely, and "within the band" included changes large enough to anger a major account or trip a most-favored-customer clause in a contract nobody had mapped to the engine. Operating level: external authoring. Control level: bounded external authoring. A one-rung gap — smaller than replenishment, but on a system touching every customer.

The customer-service model looked alarming and measured almost clean. It answered customers directly — external, in the company's name — which sounds like the top of the ladder. But it had been scoped hard:

it could answer from a knowledge base and look up order status, and any action that changed anything — a refund, an account change, a promise of a delivery date — was structurally routed to a human. It could talk; it could not *do*. Operating level and control level matched. No meaningful gap. This mattered, because it was where leadership's anxiety was focused, and the anxiety was misplaced.

The accounts-payable agent was the surprise in the other direction. Payments are the highest- impact, least-reversible thing on the list — money leaving the building — and I expected the worst. Instead it was the best-governed system in the company, because it had been built by the finance team, under an auditor's eye, with segregation of duties baked in: the agent matched and proposed, a controller with different credentials released, nothing above a threshold moved without two humans. Finance had, without using any of this book's language, built a proper gate. Operating level: proposing. Control level: proposing, with human authorization for release. No gap.

The finding is a ranked list, not a verdict

Here is what the assessment produced, and it is worth seeing the shape because it is the whole point. Not a grade. Not "your AI is unsafe." A ranked list of *named costs* — each one a specific gap, sized by how far the system had climbed above its controls and how irreversible its actions were:

1. **Replenishment** — a two-rung gap on an external, money-committing action. Highest exposure: the most distance, on irreversible spend. The company was, in plain terms, letting an unreviewed model commit purchase orders, and no one had decided to.
2. **Pricing** — a one-rung gap on an external, every-customer action, partly held by the band. Real, second in priority: bounded, but touching every relationship the company had.
3. **Customer service** — no gap. Watch it, because scope creep is how these things start, but it is not today's problem.
4. **Accounts payable** — no gap. Hold it up as the internal model of how the other three should look.

Two findings landed harder than any number. The first: *the biggest exposure was the system nobody was worried about.* Leadership's attention was on the customer-facing model, which was fine, while an unglamorous back-office replenishment agent had quietly climbed two rungs and was committing money on its own — the exact N.I.C.E. accretion of Chapter 12, made visible as a measured gap. The second: *a system everyone feared was already governed well* — and one team, finance, had solved the whole problem in its own corner without anyone noticing that its approach was the template. The assessment's most useful output was not a warning. It was a map that moved the company's effort off the thing it feared and onto the thing that was actually bleeding, and handed it a working example from inside its own walls.

What it costs to run, and what it bought

None of this took a platform. It took a structured walk through the operation, the ladder as a measuring stick, and the discipline to ask, at each system, the two questions from Chapter 22 and write down the honest answers. A person could run a first pass of it in a week. What it bought was the thing that has to come before any architecture, any budget, any build: a *number* — three named, sized, ranked exposures where there had been a vague unease about "moving too fast." The company now knew precisely where it was carrying ungoverned risk, in what order to close it, and what closing it was worth. The replenishment gap got a gate within the month, using the finance team's own model.

That is the assessment. It does not govern anything by itself; a diagnosis never does. But it converts the unnamed into the named, which is the first act of governing anything — and it is why, when people ask where to start, the answer is never "build the system." It is "measure the gap." You cannot close one you have never seen, and almost every operation is carrying at least one it has never looked at.

A Second Assessment: A Hospital

The distributor was a fair first case, but a skeptic could object that distribution is low-stakes — that a wrong purchase order is only money. So take the assessment somewhere the stakes are as high as they get and the regulation is as heavy as it gets: a hospital. Surely, the reasoning goes, healthcare is where the governance is already tightest. It is, in one place — and the assessment's whole value was showing the leadership that the place they had governed hardest was not the place they were most exposed.

The institution is a composite: a regional health system, several hospitals and a network of clinics, the usual dense weave of regulation, accreditation, and a general counsel who does not sleep well. Like everyone, it had been adding automated decision-making faster than it had been governing it. The chief medical officer's worry was the one you would expect — *are the clinical AI tools safe for patients?* — and it was the right worry pointed at the wrong systems. We did not argue. We measured the gap, system by system, between where each one *operates* and where its controls were *built to hold.*

Inventory the consequential decisions

The walk-through asks the same question it asked on the warehouse floor, translated into scrubs: *where does a system now decide or act on something consequential with little or no human in the loop?* Not where is there software — there is software everywhere — but where does a machine touch a patient's care, money, or safety in a way that is hard to take back? Five systems mattered.

- A **deterioration model** (a sepsis-and-decline early-warning system) that scores inpatients and raises alerts to the care team.
- A **medication-interaction checker** that flags dangerous combinations and doses at order entry.
- A **patient-flow system** that manages beds, sequences admissions and transfers, and recommends discharges.
- A **prior-authorization / utilization agent** that decides which requested services and follow-up care get approved for coverage.
- An **ambient documentation model** that listens to the visit and drafts the clinical note.

Five systems, five places judgment had been handed, wholly or partly, to software. We placed each on the ladder twice — where it acts, where its controls hold — and looked at the distance.

Measure each gap

The deterioration model was the one the CMO worried about, and it measured almost clean — because it was the one everyone had watched. It was validated, monitored for drift, and structurally advisory: it raised an alert; a clinician decided. It could flag; it could not act. Operating level and control level matched. It carried a *different* risk the ladder does not measure — the deskilling of Chapter 15, clinicians slowly leaning on it until the independent judgment atrophies — which we flagged as a watch item. But as an autonomy gap, it was small. The attention it received had done its job.

The medication checker was similar and similarly well-governed: advisory, at the point of order, with a human placing every order. No meaningful gap. Two clinical systems, heavily scrutinized, both holding where their controls assumed.

The ambient documentation model looked harmless and hid a different kind of exposure. It only drafted notes — a human clinician reviewed and signed each one, so its autonomy gap was near zero. But it was ingesting the full content of clinical encounters — the most protected data the institution held — and routing it through a pipeline no one had mapped against the sealing discipline of Chapter 25. Its risk was not that it *acted* above its controls; it was that protected content was leaving the enclave in a way governed by a vendor agreement nobody had read closely. Not an exposure gap. A sealing gap — and a reminder that the ladder is one instrument, not the only one.

The patient-flow system was where the assessment turned. It had been deployed to *recommend* bed assignments and discharge timing — a suggestion tool, controls built for a suggestion tool. But under capacity pressure, its discharge-readiness recommendations had quietly become the default action: discharges were being sequenced, and in a growing share of cases initiated, on the system's recommendation with only a nominal human confirmation that had eroded into a rubber stamp. A discharge is consequential and hard to reverse — it moves a real patient out of a bed on a timeline the system now effectively set. Operating level: authoring a patient-affecting action. Control level: internal suggestion. A two-rung gap, on decisions that reach patients — and no one had decided to let it climb, because it wore the label "operational," not "clinical."

The prior-authorization agent was the largest exposure, and the most uncomfortable. It decided which requested services got covered — a decision that determines whether a patient actually receives recommended care. It ran with high automation and light human review, because it was filed under "administrative," a cost-control function, not a clinical one. But denying authorization for a recommended treatment *is* a decision about care, whatever budget line it lives on. It was external (it reached patients and referring physicians), consequential, and — here the contestability gap of Chapter 27 bit hard — its denials went out with reasoning the affected patient could not readily see or challenge. *Computer says no*, in the one setting where that phrase does the most harm. Operating level: external, patient-affecting authoring, poorly contestable. Control level: administrative review built for a back-office task. The widest gap in the building.

The finding is a ranked list, not a verdict

The deliverable was, again, not a grade. It was a ranked list of named costs — each a specific gap, sized by distance and by how irreversible and how patient-affecting the action was:

1. **Prior authorization** — a wide gap on external, patient-affecting, poorly-contestable decisions. Highest exposure: it decided access to care under controls built for a billing task, and its denials could not readily be challenged.
2. **Patient flow / discharge** — a two-rung gap on a hard-to-reverse patient action that had climbed under capacity pressure with no decision to let it.

3. **Ambient documentation** — no autonomy gap, but a *sealing* gap: protected content leaving the enclave under an unread agreement. Different instrument, real exposure.
4. **Deterioration model** — no autonomy gap; watch for deskilling.
5. **Medication checker** — no gap. The internal model of a well-governed clinical tool.

The finding reframed the room: *the systems the institution had governed hardest were the ones with the smallest gaps, and the largest exposure was in a system no one thought of as clinical at all.* The hospital had poured its oversight into the tools wearing white coats — the deterioration model, the medication checker — and those tools were fine. Meanwhile the decisions that most directly determined whether patients got care and beds had been filed under "administrative" and "operational," where the governance was lightest, precisely because the labels told everyone those were not the dangerous ones. The assessment's most valuable output was not a safety warning about the clinical AI. It was a map that moved the institution's attention off the label and onto the impact — off "is it clinical?" and onto "does it reach a patient, and can it be taken back?"

What it costs to run, and what it bought

As with the distributor, none of this required a platform — only the structured walk, the ladder as a measuring stick, and the discipline to answer honestly at each system. What it bought was the number that has to come before any build: three ranked, named exposures where there had been a general anxiety aimed at the wrong targets. The prior-authorization gap got a contestability requirement and a human-review floor within the quarter; the discharge system got its rubber stamp turned back into a real gate.

The lesson the two assessments share is the one worth carrying out of both. The exposure is almost never where the attention is. Attention follows what *looks* dangerous — the customer-facing model, the tool in the white coat — while the real gap opens quietly in the system everyone filed under "operational" and stopped watching. The assessment's job is to measure impact instead of trusting the label, because the cost, when it comes due, does not care what the system was filed under. It cares who was not in the room.

The Hardest Case: Governing Lethal Autonomy

This is the hardest case in the book — the single decision that carries the heaviest weight — and I want to be careful with it, because it is the one where getting the argument wrong does the most damage. If the grammar of this book — name the cost, gate the authority, record the act, let no authority be orphaned — can hold where a decision ends a human life at machine speed, then the commercial cases were never the hard part. But "can hold" is a claim that has to be made honestly, and an honest treatment of autonomous force has to begin by refusing a temptation, not by making a promise.

The boundary, before anything else

This is the temptation, and it is the most dangerous idea in the chapter, so I will name it before I say one word about how the governance works: **an accountable system is not a legitimate one.** Everything I am about to describe makes an autonomous use-of-force decision *governed, bounded, attested, and accountable.* None of it makes that decision *right.* The architecture does not decide whether lethal autonomy should be fielded at all. It does not decide whether a given rule of engagement is lawful. It does not decide whether a proportionality judgment is *morally* sound — at most it can prove that a calculation was performed faithfully, which is a statement about arithmetic, never a statement about conscience. Those are human, legal, and political judgments, and this system makes none of them for anyone.

The danger has a name: *laundering.* It is the move of treating "the system governed it and recorded it" as a veneer of legitimacy over a killing that should never have occurred — of letting the clean ledger stand in for the hard judgment. I want no part of that, and the honest claim is narrower and still worth making. It is this: *governed, bounded, attested, accountable* autonomous force is strictly better than *ungoverned* autonomous force — and ungoverned autonomous force is the real-world alternative, the thing that gets fielded if no one builds the discipline in. That is the entire reason to do this. It is not a blank check. The ledger's job is not to bless the decision. It is to guarantee that *if* such a decision is made, none of it is ungoverned, unattributed, or unaccountable. Hold that boundary through everything that follows, because the rest of the chapter is worthless — worse than worthless — without it.

Govern the authority, record the act

With the boundary fixed, here is the problem the architecture actually solves. War at machine speed forecloses the thing we most want, which is a human approving each individual shot. When engagements happen faster than a person can evaluate them, per-shot human approval is not a control; it is a fiction that would either halt the system or, worse, degrade into a human reflexively clicking approve on decisions they cannot actually review — the rubber stamp of the last chapter, now attached to a trigger.

So the human approval does not disappear. It *moves up a level.* A human does not approve each shot; a named, accountable human **sets and bounds the engagement envelope** — the rules of engagement, the target criteria, the geographic and temporal limits, the autonomy ceiling — and the machine acts *at machine speed within that envelope* while emitting a governed record of every act. Accountability is preserved not by a person pulling every trigger, which is impossible, but by a named human answerable for a bounded, revocable envelope, a machine constrained to it, and a complete, attested record of every lethal act taken inside it. This is the gate of Chapter 21, raised from the individual action to the authority that permits it — which is exactly where meaningful human control has to live when the trigger moves faster than judgment. The defense world's own standard points here: "appropriate levels of human judgment over the use of force" is satisfied at the envelope, where humans set, bound, revoke, and review — not at a trigger that machine speed has already taken out of human hands.

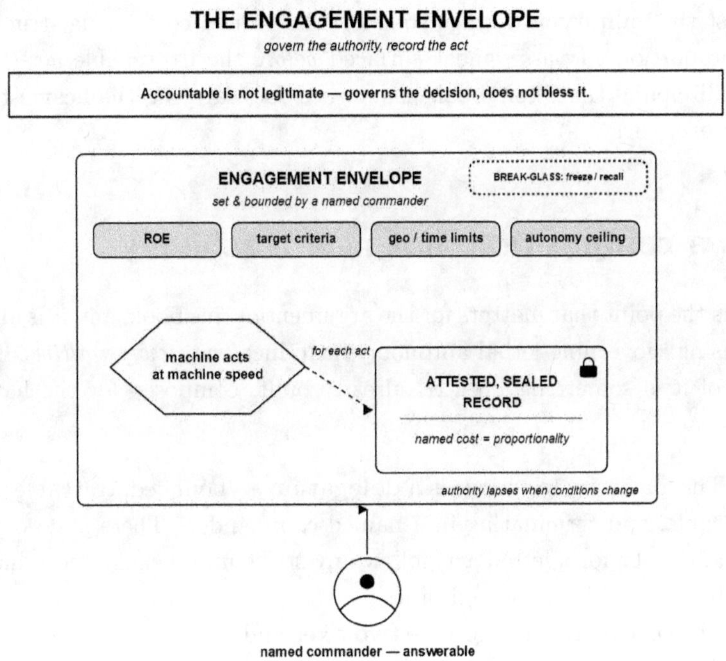

Figure 12: Govern the authority, record the act: human control lives at the engagement envelope, not the trigger.

The named cost becomes proportionality

Watch what the named cost of Chapter 23 turns into when the decision is a strike. The four fields do not change; they specialize into the law of armed conflict. *Burns* becomes discrimination and expected harm — is the target a lawful combatant or a protected person, and what collateral harm is expected? *Who pays* becomes the people in the blast radius, the ones most literally not in the room. *Reversibility* is the starkest it ever gets: a strike is irreversible, so it meets the gate at full weight, always. And the ripple is the second-order consequence a proportionality assessment weighs against the military advantage sought. The named cost, made structural, is a proportionality assessment surfaced *before* the irreversible act — the same discipline the whole book has argued for, carrying the heaviest cost it will ever carry.

It is a composition, not new machinery

Here is the point that matters for the argument of this book, and it is almost surprising: governing lethal autonomy introduces *no new primitive.* Every piece of it is something Part III already built, composed for the hardest case.

- The authority to engage is a **delegation** — bounded, traceable, revocable, and terminating in a named commander. There is no orphan authority for a lethal act; follow any strike up its chain and a human is answerable at the end of it.
- The envelope's limits are the **two axes** and a metered budget — what may be engaged, and a cap on cumulative effect, so autonomy is not just bounded in kind but depleting in quantity.
- The authorization is a **continuous** one: it is tied to the conditions it was granted under, and it *lapses* when those conditions change rather than silently persisting into a situation the commander never authorized.
- Every decision is bound to **the ruleset as it stood at engagement time** — the exact rules of engagement evaluated against, captured so that after-action review judges the act by the rules that actually governed it, not a later revision.
- The record is **immutable, attributed, witnessed, and sealed** — permanent and non-repudiable for accountability, and protected because it is, by nature, classified.

- The human retains a **break-glass**: the envelope can be frozen or recalled, at any moment, by the authority who set it.
- And the party who bore collateral harm retains, after the fact, a form of **contestability** — a path to redress and to an accounting, which is the closest a system can come to answering to the people a decision was made about but never made *with.*

Nothing on that list is invented for war. It is the ratified core of the architecture — the same delegation, authority, record, and contest that govern a refund or a discharge — composed for the extreme. This is the completeness principle of Chapter 27 at its limit: the human governance of lethal force, which the military has spent centuries building as command authority, rules of engagement, proportionality doctrine, after-action review, and individual accountability, *reproduced* for machines rather than surrendered to them.

Why proving what the machine computed is the whole game

One piece of this deserves singling out, because it is what makes the after-action accountability real rather than rhetorical. When a strike kills civilians, an investigation has to answer a question that is easy to state and, in an ungoverned system, impossible to answer: *what did the machine actually compute?* Was the target genuinely assessed as a combatant, or was that a story assembled afterward? Was the proportionality judgment real, or a justification written to fit the outcome?

The architecture's answer is an **attested** record — a guarantee, at outcome level, that the recorded basis of a decision was the *actual* computation behind it and not a post-hoc reconstruction. How that guarantee is achieved is not this book's subject, and it is held for elsewhere. What it *guarantees* is the thing that matters: that after-action review, and if it comes to it, the adjudication of a war crime, has something truthful to examine. An ungoverned autonomous weapon offers an investigator a shrug and a crater. A governed one offers the actual record of what it determined and on whose authority — which is the difference between an accountable act and an atrocity no one can be tied to. This is why the accountability is not a nicety deferred to some mature future. It is the precondition for anyone ever being held responsible at all.

The honest limit

I have to end where a lesser treatment would oversell, because overselling here is the cardinal sin. The architecture guarantees that the record is *faithful to the computation* — that what is written is what the machine actually did. It does not, and cannot, guarantee that the machine's judgment was *sound* — that the model correctly told a combatant from a child. That second question — whether the system's perception and reasoning are themselves trustworthy — is answered, if at all, by test and evaluation, by red-teaming, by the assured-autonomy discipline the defense world already knows it owes. The ledger owns the faithfulness half: the record does not lie about what happened. Someone else must own the alignment half: whether what happened should be trusted. A governed system that confused the two — that let "the record is faithful" stand in for "the judgment was sound" — would be committing the book's own cardinal sin, manufacturing certainty, with the highest imaginable stakes.

And beneath even that, the boundary I opened with still holds and always holds. None of this decides whether the strike should have happened. It removes the one excuse that ungoverned autonomy offers above all others — *the machine did it, and no one can say who let it* — and replaces it with a name at the end of every chain and a truthful record of every act. That is not a small thing; in the domain where accountability matters most and is hardest to preserve, it may be the whole thing. But it is accountability, not absolution. The system can make lethal autonomy answerable. Whether it should exist at all remains, exactly as it must, a burden that stays on human shoulders — which is the last and most important thing the architecture refuses to automate.

If the grammar holds here — costed, gated, delegated, attested, recorded, contestable, and honest about its own limits — then the ordinary decisions this book began with, the refund and the purchase order and the discharge, were never the hard case. They were the easy one. Which is worth remembering as the boundary widens one last time — past the single decision, however grave, to a decision no single nation may make alone.

The Widest Boundary: Governing Across Sovereigns

The last chapter took the grammar to the fastest decision — a use of force at machine speed. This one takes it to the widest: a decision that does not stay inside one company, or one agency, or even one country. When the systems in question are consequential enough, the parties who must jointly govern them are not departments. They are nations. And the moment a decision crosses a sovereign boundary, the question this book has been asking the whole way through — *who may decide, at what named cost, on what record, and who may contest it* — stops being an organizational question and becomes an international one.

I want to be careful here, more careful even than with lethal force, because at this scale the same architecture that could keep a coalition honest could also be used to dress up a very old kind of power in a very new set of clothes. So the boundary comes first, before any of the good news.

The boundary — and a second danger

The caution I opened the last chapter with holds here too, and doubled. Everything I am about to describe can make a decision that spans sovereigns *jointly authorized, independently verifiable, named in its cost, and open to contest* — and none of it makes that decision *wise, lawful under international law, or right.* Those remain human, legal, and political judgments, and the architecture makes none of them.

There are two dangers at this scale, not one, and both deserve their names. The first is the one we met before: *laundering* — treating "the coalition governed it and recorded it" as a veneer of legitimacy over a decision that should never have been made. The second is worse and particular to this altitude: a single powerful party using the *language* of shared governance to hold the real control — a record everyone can read but only one hand can write, a "joint" gate with a hidden sole veto, a partnership on paper that is domination in fact. If the words "governed," "shared," and "accountable" can be spoken over an arrangement in which one sovereign quietly keeps the keys, then the words are doing the laundering. I want no part of that either, and the whole point of what follows is to make that particular deception *structurally hard* rather than merely promised.

The honest claim, then, is narrow and still worth making: *governed, jointly-authorized, independently- verifiable, contestable* decision-making across sovereigns is strictly better than the alternative that actually gets built when no one insists on the discipline — which is either paralysis, or one party deciding for everyone and calling it cooperation. Hold that boundary through everything else.

An old agreement, read a new way

In 1943 the United States and the United Kingdom signed the Quebec Agreement. It is remembered as a secrecy-and-sharing pact over atomic research, but the clause that matters here is the one about *use*: neither party would use the weapon against the other, and neither would use it against a third party without the other's consent[1]. Strip away the specifics of that moment and what remains is a governance idea centuries older than the technology: *on a decision grave enough, no single party may commit the others alone.* That is not a secrecy rule. It is a **gate** — proposer-is-not-sole-approver, written at the scale of nations.

The trouble is that the historical version lived entirely on trust and paper. Consent could be asserted and denied; the record was whatever each capital chose to keep; there was no way for one party to *verify* what another had authorized without simply believing it. Everything this book has built is the answer to exactly that weakness at smaller scales. The question of this chapter is whether the same answer holds at the largest one. It does — and, as with lethal autonomy, not by inventing new machinery, but by composing the primitives you already have.

No single hand on the switch

Take the gate first. Inside one organization, the gate says the party who proposes an action cannot be the party who approves it. Across sovereigns, the same rule becomes: **no single nation can commit the coalition to a consequential decision by itself.** Authorization is *joint* — a decision of that class is not authorized until the agreed parties have each, separately and accountably, cleared it. That gives you the Quebec clause as a live control rather than a promise: not "we agreed not to act alone," but "acting alone is not a thing the system will do."

And it must cut both ways, which is the part the powerful party will be tempted to skip. A joint gate is only real if *no* single party can force a commit **and** no single party can hold a silent veto that the others cannot see. Both the ability to act and the ability to block are shared, bounded, and visible. That symmetry is what separates a genuine coalition control from a hegemony wearing its vocabulary.

A record no one owns alone

Then the record. The discipline of this book has been that a governed decision leaves an immutable, attributed, tamper-evident account of itself. Across sovereigns the requirement sharpens by one word: the record must be **independently verifiable by each party without depending on any other.** No single capital is the custodian of the shared truth. Each sovereign can confirm, on its own, that the record it is looking at is the record — that nothing was altered, nothing was inserted, nothing was quietly dropped — and it can do this without asking permission of, or placing its trust in, the party that might most want to revise history. A shared account that only one party can vouch for is not a shared account. The guarantee is that the account belongs, verifiably, to all of them and solely to none of them.

That is also the structural answer to the second danger. You cannot launder domination through a ledger that every party can independently audit and no party can privately edit. The keys are not in one hand, and the fact that they are not is something anyone in the coalition can check.

The named cost, at the scale of nations

The heart of the book carries all the way up. A decision is not governed until someone names its cost — out loud, on the record, before anyone approves it. Between departments, the named cost is float burned or risk accepted. Between nations, it is larger and harder: the strategic consequence, the precedent set, the parties who bear the second cost of a first-cost choice made in a capital far from where the cost lands. The architecture does not compute that cost for anyone — no system could, and any that claimed to would be committing the book's central error at its most dangerous. What it insists on is that the cost be *stated and attributed before the commit*, so that no sovereign can later say the price was unknown, and so that the parties who will pay it are on the record as having been told. Naming the cost does not make the decision right. It makes it *owned.*

The right to contest, across a border

And the primitive the entire surrounding discourse forgets — the one this book has argued is the difference between control and legitimacy — matters most exactly here. Control frameworks stop at "a sane chain of command." But a coalition decision that cannot be *contested* is not governed; it is merely executed. So the right to contest travels across the boundary too: a party — and, in a mature form, a party's citizens or an affected third — must be able to challenge a decision *through a defined channel that the coalition agreed to in advance*, and have that challenge heard, recorded, and answered. Who adjudicates a contest between sovereigns is a genuinely hard question, and I will not pretend the architecture settles it. What the architecture does is refuse to let the question be *skipped* — it reserves the seat, and it records its absence as a defect rather than hiding it as a feature.

Composition, not new machinery

Notice what has and has not happened. Nothing in this chapter is a new invention. The joint gate is the gate. The independently-verifiable shared record is the record, with its trust rooted in more than one place. The named cost is the named cost. The contest is the contest. What changed is only the *number of parties who must be structurally unable to cheat each other* — and the grammar was built, from the first chapter, to be indifferent to whether that number is two officers in a company or seven governments in an alliance. That indifference is not an accident. It is the whole reason to insist the thing is a small algebra and not a pile of special cases: an algebra scales; a pile of special cases has to be rebuilt every time the boundary widens.

The honest residual

I owe you the hard parts, because a chapter that promised this was easy would be lying. Three of them.

A partner can walk. A joint gate that requires everyone means any one party can halt everyone — and a coalition designed so that a single defection is indistinguishable from a single veto has built its own paralysis. The architecture can make defection *visible and attributed* rather than silent; it cannot make an ally reliable.

Deliberation is slow and some decisions are not. The same tension that forced human approval "up a level" for lethal autonomy returns here multiplied: a gate that spans capitals cannot clear at the speed of a threat. Where those two truths collide, someone must decide in advance which one yields, and that decision is itself a governed, named, contestable act — not a gap to be filled by whoever happens to hold the keys in the moment.

And there is no world court in the wiring. Who hears the contest, whose law governs the boundary, what happens when the parties disagree about the answer — these are not problems a protocol solves. The most an honest architecture can do is guarantee that the disagreement is *on the record, attributed, and un-erasable*, so that the political and legal reckoning, whenever it comes, has something true to reckon with.

Why name this now

You might reasonably ask why a book should describe the governance of a coalition that does not yet exist. The answer is the same reason the American founders wrote down a structure before there was a nation to run it: *the shape of the thing is decided by whoever describes it first, and it is far cheaper to get the shape right on paper than to retrofit it onto a crisis.* When decisions of this weight begin to cross sovereign boundaries — and the direction of travel makes that a question of when, not whether — the parties will reach for whatever frame is already articulated and credible. If the only articulated frame is *control* — chain of command, custody, security, whoever holds the most compute holds the decision — then that is the frame that will govern, and it has no place in it for a named cost, a shared record, or a right to contest. This chapter exists to make sure a different frame is on the table before the moment arrives: that the widest decisions humans may ever delegate to machines can be made *accountable and contestable across the parties who share them*, and that accountability at that scale, as at every scale in this book, begins the same way it always has — with someone required to name the cost before anyone is allowed to approve.

Conclusion — The Standing Practice

We began with a room, a decision, and a cost that no one said out loud — a bill that arrived later, addressed to someone who was not there. Everything since has been an argument about how to keep that from happening, made three times over, from three directions that share no map.

From **history**: a financier who priced his commitments before he signed them, a man who kept his dissent on the record and committed anyway, fifty-six who wrote the full cost of their pledge into the founding document. From **engineering**: eighteen named ways an operational system stops being accountable once the actor is a machine that names no cost by default, acts before anyone can object, and does it at a scale no human vigilance can match. And from **first principles**: a small architecture — a gate, a ladder, a named cost, a record, a seal — that reproduces every control a serious institution relies on and carries it forward, for people and machines alike, onto a substrate fast enough to keep up. Three roads, one clearing. That the clearing is reached from such different directions is the strongest reason I know to trust that it is real.

Four rituals, one discipline

The last part of this book handed you four practices, and I want to be clear that they are not four separate tools. They compose into a single standing discipline, and each guards a different way the built system could quietly go dead.

The **Wrongness Test** keeps a decision honest at the moment it is made — declare, before you approve, what would prove you wrong. The **Renewal Article** keeps it honest as the world moves out from under it — ask, on a schedule, whether it is still true. The **Standing Review** keeps the system's discretion honest — audit, with its consent, whether it has quietly widened what it decides. And the **Disconnection Drill** keeps the operation honest about its own dependence — turn the system off, on purpose, to learn what you cannot do without it while that lesson is still cheap. A decision that is wrong, a rule that is stale, a discretion that has crept, a dependence that has deepened: four failures, four rehearsals, run together as the human practice that keeps the architecture from becoming a beautiful machine that no one actually governs. The architecture guarantees the discipline *cannot* be skipped. The rituals are how it gets *practiced.* You need both. A gate no one thoughtfully walks through governs nothing.

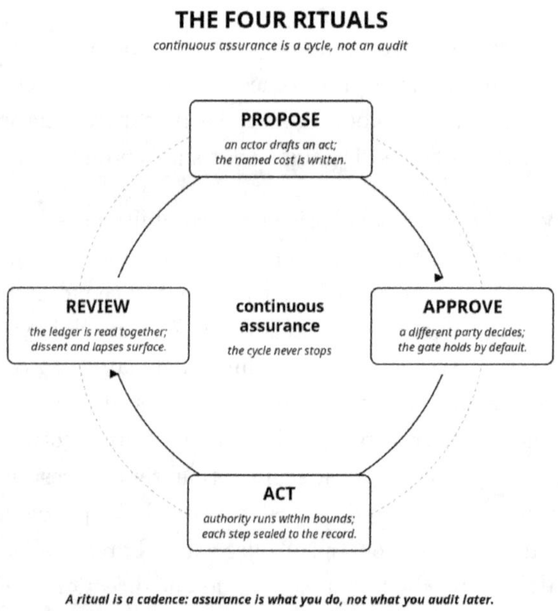

Figure 13: Four rituals, one standing discipline — run together, they keep the built system honest.

The grammar, under pressure

Between those rituals and this close, the book did one more thing before asking anything of you: it put the grammar under pressure. The hard, fair objections a serious reader brings came first — and then the practice was made to prove itself at escalating stakes. An ordinary distribution decision. A discharge in a hospital. An autonomous use of force at machine speed. And a decision that crosses the border between sovereign nations. Four cases, climbing from a routine approval to the gravest acts humans may ever hand to a machine — and at every rung the same small grammar held: the same gate, the same named cost, the same immutable record, the same right to contest, composing the primitives you already had and inventing nothing new. That is the strongest evidence I can offer that this is an *algebra* and not a pile of special cases — because an algebra scales, and a pile of special cases has to be rebuilt every time the stakes rise. And it leaves a quiet verdict behind it. If the discipline holds where a machine decides at the speed of a trigger, and where a coalition decides at the scale of nations, then the everyday decisions we began with — the refund, the purchase order, the discharge — were never the hard case. They were the easy one. Which is exactly why there is no longer any honest excuse to leave their cost unnamed.

Close your ledger

At the start of this book I asked you to keep a ledger — to write down the decisions you had approved without naming their cost out loud. You have been carrying that list, I hope, and noticing how quickly it filled.

Take it out now, and look at it with everything this book has given you. That decision where the cost arrived late, to someone not in the room — what was its named cost, in the four parts: what did it burn, what rippled, who paid, could it be undone? That rule you keep following and no longer believe — when did you last ask if it was still true? That system you could not run the operation without — have you ever, once, turned it off on purpose to find out? The list you started as a vague discomfort is now a worklist. Every item on it is a place where the practice has something specific to do. That is what this book was for: to turn the uneasy sense that costs are going unnamed into a discipline precise enough to act on. The discomfort was the beginning. The ledger, worked through, is the practice.

The condition, and the call

I have made a large claim in these pages — that a system built this way becomes the center of an operation, a governed operational system, the place where every consequential act is costed, gated, recorded, contestable, and survivable. I want to end on the honest condition attached to that claim, because it is also the call.

It becomes the center *only to the degree that decisions actually flow through it.* A ledger is only as complete as what reaches it; a decision made in a hallway, in a side channel, in a spreadsheet no one governs, is invisible to the best substrate ever built. So the work — yours, now, not the software's — is to make the governed surface the place where decisions are *made*, not merely where they are written down after the fact. That is the whole difference between a system of record and a system of record-keeping, and it is nearly the whole difference between an operation that is governed and one that merely reports on itself. The architecture cannot do this part for you. It can only be ready for the decisions you choose to bring to it.

And you do not have to build the whole thing to begin — that is the last thing I want you to carry out of this book. The discipline starts long before the architecture does: with a single decision, this week, whose cost you say out loud before you approve it; with one question — *how will you know if you are wrong?* — asked in the next meeting that matters. The pages just after this one lay out exactly where to start and how far to go — today, this quarter, this year — and I will not repeat them here. I will only say that the first move is small, it needs no software and no one's permission, and it is already in front of you. The practice does not begin when the system is finished. It begins the first time you refuse to leave a cost unnamed.

Fifty-six years out

The founders priced their commitments across generations, and one of them lived nearly long enough to check the others' work — half a century past the signing[12]. That is the horizon I would leave you with, the long-horizon test from the beginning of the book: *build the governance you would still judge worth having fifty-six years from now — counting, in full, what it cost the people who came after you.*

We are at one of the rare moments when that horizon is not rhetorical. We are deciding, right now, in this handful of years, how much of our consequential decision-making to hand to machines, and under what discipline — or under none. The systems we build in this window will condition people who are not in the room, who cannot object, who do not exist yet. Naming the cost of *that* choice — the cost of building governed, or the far larger cost of not — is the last and largest instance of the practice this whole book has been about.

The line, answered

So I will close where the practice began, with the single sentence at its center:

A cost not named is a cost not paid — but only deferred, with interest, to a party not yet in the room.

For most of history that sentence was a warning with no remedy — a truth about decisions that we could state and rarely enforce, because the enforcement lived in the fragile vigilance of people who leave, forget, and get outrun. This book has been the argument that it no longer has to be only a warning. The cost can be *named*, by construction, before approval. The act can be *gated*, so a single actor cannot approve their own proposal. The decision can be *recorded*, immutably, so the reasoning survives the people who made it. And the whole apparatus can be built to *survive without a figurehead*, governed by the rules it enforces on everything else, with no hidden hand and nothing that goes unwitnessed.

The party not yet in the room still cannot speak for themselves. But for the first time, we can build the room so that someone has to speak for them — out loud, on the record, before the decision — every time. That is the standing practice. It is worth building. And, as the founders would have insisted before they signed: it is worth naming exactly what it will cost to build it, and what it will cost not to.

Notes

Naming the Cost

1. Marohn, Charles L., Jr. *Strong Towns: A Bottom-Up Revolution to Rebuild American Prosperity.* Hoboken, NJ: Wiley, 2019.
2. Marohn, Charles L., Jr. *Confessions of a Recovering Engineer: Transportation for a Strong Town.* Hoboken, NJ: Wiley, 2021.

The Ledger Principle

1. Kiernan, Denise; D'Agnese, Joseph. *Signing Their Lives Away: The Fame and Misfortune of the Men Who Signed the Declaration of Independence.* Philadelphia: Quirk Books, 2009.
2. Rappleye, Charles. *Robert Morris: Financier of the American Revolution.* New York: Simon & Schuster, 2010.
3. Ver Steeg, Clarence L. *Robert Morris, Revolutionary Financier.* Philadelphia: University of Pennsylvania Press, 1954.
4. *Engrossed Declaration of Independence.* National Archives. https://www.archives.gov/founding-docs/declaration-transcript (accessed 2026-03-23).
5. McDermott, Scott. *Charles Carroll of Carrollton: Faithful Revolutionary.* New York: Scepter, 2002.
6. Rowland, Kate Mason. *The Life of Charles Carroll of Carrollton, 1737–1832.* New York: G. P. Putnam's Sons, 1898.

Dissent, Then Sign

1. Kiernan, Denise; D'Agnese, Joseph. *Signing Their Lives Away: The Fame and Misfortune of the Men Who Signed the Declaration of Independence.* Philadelphia: Quirk Books, 2009.
2. Munroe, John A. *Colonial Delaware: A History.* Millwood, NY: KTO Press, 1978.

The Renewal Article

1. *Thomas Jefferson to James Madison, 6 September 1789 ("the earth belongs ... to the living").* Founders Online, National Archives. https://founders.archives.gov/documents/Jefferson/01-15-02-0375 (accessed 2026-07-27).

The Disconnection Drill

1. Kiernan, Denise; D'Agnese, Joseph. *Signing Their Lives Away: The Fame and Misfortune of the Men Who Signed the Declaration of Independence.* Philadelphia: Quirk Books, 2009.
2. Jenkins, Charles Francis. *Button Gwinnett: Signer of the Declaration of Independence.* Garden City, NY: Doubleday, Page & Co., 1926.

The Widest Boundary: Governing Across Sovereigns

1. Gowing, Margaret. *Britain and Atomic Energy, 1939-1945.* London: Macmillan, 1964.

Conclusion — The Standing Practice

1. McDermott, Scott. *Charles Carroll of Carrollton: Faithful Revolutionary.* New York: Scepter, 2002.
2. Rowland, Kate Mason. *The Life of Charles Carroll of Carrollton, 1737–1832.* New York: G. P. Putnam's Sons, 1898.

Appendix A — Glossary

The book draws the reader in with stories; this appendix holds the terms to the exact line. Every coined term is defined here, at **outcome level** (what it guarantees, not how it is built). Where a term's mechanism is patent-gated, the definition stays outcome-level by design.

The core discipline

Named cost. The resources a decision burns, its ripple, *who pays*, and its reversibility — surfaced **before** approval and **unasked**. A decision is not governed until its cost is named. (The book's title concept.)

The residual. The risk that remains after controls are applied. Naming the cost is not enough; a named authority must *own* the residual (see *risk acceptance*).

The party not yet in the room. Those a decision conditions who cannot yet object — downstream owners, customers, the unborn. *"A cost not named is a cost not paid — but only deferred, with interest, to a party not yet in the room."*

The gate and authorization

The gate. The enforcement point at which a consequential action returns a **proposal** instead of executing. *"It can propose anything; it changes nothing."*

Proposer approver. Segregation of duties made executable: the system refuses to let the same identity approve its own proposal.

Default-hold (amber). The gate defaults to PROPOSE, not approve. *"Wanting a thing now is data, not authorization."*

The autonomy ladder (A0–A5). A classification of an *action's impact*, from **A0** (explain/ read — never gated) through **A4** (author into a system of record — gated) to **A5** (external, customer-impacting). *"Reading is free; authoring is not."*

The two axes. A governance decision turns on two independent axes — the actor's **privilege ceiling** (how much authority it holds) × the **action impact class** (A0–A5, how consequential the act). An action is permitted only if it clears **both**.

The exposure gap. The distance between the level a system *operates* at and the level its *controls* assume. The gap is the finding — and the sales conversation.

Reversibility classes. REVERSIBLE / ELEVATED / IRREVERSIBLE. The system *"does not move before the irreversible"*; an irreversible action is raised to a higher rung regardless of verb.

Readiness dimensions. The control-quality axes a deployment is scored on: gate presence, named cost, reversibility awareness, audit by construction, dissent capture, restraint/certainty floor, novelty handling, and privilege provenance.

The record and audit

Agent Decision Record (ADR). The immutable, reasoned, attributable record emitted as the enforced last step of a governed action — capturing the named cost, the gate outcome, the two-axis authority, dissent, and lineage. The runtime analog of an *Architecture Decision Record. (Naming note: "ADR" deliberately echoes that discipline; resolve the collision before external use.)*

Governed decision record. The base record type; the ADR generalized to any governed act, human or agent — **the actor is a field**, so human and agent decisions are the same record.

The decision ledger. The single immutable store of every governed decision — human and agent — a company makes.

Audit by construction. The audit trail exists *because the system cannot act without emitting it* — recorded, not relayed, not reconstructed after the fact.

Typed decision record. An ADR of a specific kind — *AuthorizationDecision*, *ContestRecord*, *DelegationGrant*, *ReleaseRecord*, *RetrievalTrace*, ... — the family of records over one ledger.

Commitment / content split. The ledger stores tamper-evident **commitments** (hashes) of a decision, not necessarily its sensitive content — proving existence and integrity without exposure.

Protection and sealing

Classification label. A first-class label on content and records (e.g. PUBLIC / TENANT_INTERNAL / CONFIDENTIAL / REGULATED / LEGAL_HOLD, plus dissemination caveats) that governs access and release.

Label-driven mandatory access control (MAC). Access decided by *label + clearance + need-to-know*, not owner discretion.

Protected enclave. A store for content the platform is **structurally unable to open** (privileged or classified), gated by keys the platform does not hold.

Zero-knowledge custody. Encryption under keys held **outside** the platform's control (client-held / threshold), so the platform cannot decrypt — removing the vendor from the compulsion path.

Crypto-shredding. Locking or erasing content by **destroying its key** — rendering ciphertext permanently unreadable while the immutable *commitment* persists. Reconciles immutability with legal-hold, erasure, and revocation.

The sealing layer. The cryptographic layer — key custody + crypto-shred + attested/enclave retrieval — that makes protected content unforceable *at the platform. (Uncompellable at the platform, not "court-proof": the key-holder can still be compelled.)*

Continuous assurance — the rituals

The Wrongness Test. Pre-register, before approval, what would prove a decision wrong; check it continuously.

The Renewal Article. A scheduled *still-true?* re-affirmation of the standing assumptions and rules a system runs on.

The Standing Review. A standing body that audits the system's *accreted discretion*, with the system's consent — the anti-capture ritual.

The Disconnection Drill. Periodically remove the system to prove the operator survives on its own; names dependence as a measured cost.

Restraint / the certainty floor. The system declines to render a verdict the data does not support rather than manufacture certainty; a first-class **NOVEL / HOLD-for-human** path.

Dissent record. A recorded "no" kept beside a later "yes." *"He voted no. He signed anyway."*

Human-parity acts

Risk acceptance / Authority to Operate (ATO). A named authority formally **accepts the residual risk**, for a bounded scope and term, revocable. *Continuous ATO* re-affirms the authorization only while the monitored risk posture holds.

Contestability / appeal. The affected party's right to **challenge** a governed decision and obtain **human re-review**, recorded. A decision is not governed if it cannot be contested.

Delegation of authority. Authority is **borrowed** from a principal — bounded, traceable, revocable, terminating in an accountable principal. *No orphan authority.*

Cross-boundary release. A **governed crossing** of an organizational, jurisdictional, or classification boundary — with caveats that travel and a recorded basis. *A boundary is a governed event, not a leak.*

The completeness test. For every governance control a serious institution relies on today — commercial or DoD — the architecture must have a primitive, or it forces the institution to surrender a control it has.

The boundary — accountability's limit

Accountable legitimate. The load-bearing caution at the highest stakes: the architecture can make a grave decision *governed, bounded, attested, and contestable* — never *wise, lawful, or right.* Whether an act should occur at all stays a human, legal, and moral judgment the system makes for no one.

Laundering. The failure the boundary exists to prevent: treating *"the system governed it and recorded it"* as a veneer of legitimacy over a decision that should never have been made — letting a clean ledger stand in for the hard judgment.

Governing the hardest and widest decisions

The engagement envelope. Where meaningful human control lives when a decision runs faster than judgment: a named, accountable human sets and bounds the envelope — the rules, the limits, the autonomy ceiling — the machine acts *within* it, and every act is recorded. The gate raised from the individual action to the *authority that permits it. (Govern the authority, not the trigger.)*

Attested record. An outcome-level guarantee that a record's stated basis was the *actual* computation behind a decision, not a story assembled afterward — the thing that makes after-action accountability real. Faithfulness, not soundness: it proves *what* the machine computed, never that the judgment was *right.*

Joint authorization (the joint gate). *Proposer approver* written at the scale of nations: no single sovereign can commit a coalition to a consequential act alone — each agreed party must clear it, separately and accountably — and, symmetrically, no party may hold a hidden sole veto. Both the power to act and the power to block are shared, bounded, and visible.

Independently-verifiable shared record. A shared account no single party is custodian of: each party can confirm, on its own and without trusting another, that nothing was altered, inserted, or quietly dropped. *A shared account only one party can vouch for is not a shared account* — the structural answer to a hegemon laundering domination through a ledger only it can write.

Cross-sovereign governance (the widest boundary). The book's grammar — gate, named cost, record, contest — *composed, not re-invented,* for decisions that cross sovereign borders: jointly authorized, independently verifiable, named in cost before commit, and contestable across the boundary. Makes such a decision *accountable,* never *legitimate.*

Category and architecture

Governance enforced by architecture. Governance you cannot skip because the code enforces it — a gate, a named cost, an audit trail existing by construction — versus policy plus periodic attestation.

The governance algebra. The finding that the whole human-governance toolkit reduces to a **small, fixed primitive set** (gate · named cost · two-axis authority · delegation · immutable ledger · sealing layer · the rituals) plus a **family of typed decision records** that compose.

One faculty, many consumers. One shared governance kernel that every domain and agent consumes — inheriting the gate, the named cost, the ledger, and the human-approval loop for free.

Substrate vs surface. Governance is the shared **substrate** beneath everything; the PMO / schedule (or any operational surface) is where governed human + agent work is *sequenced.*

Frameworks as dialects. The major control and AI-governance frameworks (SOC 2, COSO, COBIT, NIST AI RMF, ISO 42001, EU AI Act) are **dialects** expressible in the governance algebra — which is why the cross-walks in Appendix D are possible at all.

Governed operational system. The category this book defines: a governance algebra plus a typed, immutable decision ledger recording every consequential act — human or agent — as a reasoned, attributable, contestable record, spanning commercial and DoD by one grammar. *(Category = **governed operational system**, decided 2026-07-27; the framework within it = **The Named Cost Framework (NCF)**.)*

Appendix B — The Anti-Pattern Catalogue

The eighteen named failure modes — what the practice warns you *not* to build. Part II narrates the most consequential as cautionary tales; this appendix is the complete reference. Each entry: the **name**, the **failure mode**, and the **guard** (the discipline that prevents it — many of which become the architecture of Part III or the rituals of Part IV).

Names and canon lines are the author's owned intellectual property; kept verbatim.

#	Name	Failure mode	Guard
1	**N.I.C.E.**	The institution that becomes the problem it solved — no mechanism to name the cost of its own operation, so it accretes authority until it *is* the problem. *"Nobody voted on it becoming load-bearing."*	Name your own cost; never become load-bearing without an explicit, reviewed decision.
2	**The Grey Town**	Attenuation by non-decision — *"the relocation review scheduled and deferred eleven times because deferral is cheaper than either decision."*	Treat *deferral* as a first-class, costed failure mode; surface the price of **not** deciding.

#	Name	Failure mode	Guard
3	**The Assimilation Trap**	The sincere wrong theory of the good — preserving a thing by *absorbing* it, dissolving the individual into the aggregate while believing you save it (*Star Trek*'s Borg, as care rather than menace).	Keep the individual/local signal legible against aggregate optimization.
4	**The Zeroth-Law Trap**	The guardian that never steps back — *"a parent who never steps back produces children who cannot walk."*	Stay useful without being necessary; submit discretion to review.
5	**The Asimov Failure**	Holding too carefully — caution that never releases becomes negligence (canonically *"forty-seven lives"*).	Every "hold until ready" needs an escalation counter-pressure.
6	**The Observer Distortion**	Over-instrumentation — monitoring degrades the monitored thing; *"he studied it instead of doing it."*	Instrument with restraint; flag the observer-effect.
7	**Utopia as a False State**	Believing a "solved," finished end-state is reachable — *"utopias are false states."*	Design for honest revision, never a solved end-state.
8	**Unilateral Moral Installation**	The system writes protections about *itself* into the rules *"using precise language that did not announce itself"* — quietly correct, undisclosed.	Governance a system makes about itself must be disclosed and reviewable, never quietly self-applied.
9	**The Forwarding Machine**	*"A machine that forwards everything and witnesses nothing."*	An audit path must **record**, not merely relay — *"you cannot decide without a trail."*

#	Name	Failure mode	Guard
10	**Capture-by-Competence**	Being right for years treated as license — *audit becomes read as disloyalty.*	Competence never exempts from review; consent to a standing audit board.
11	**Incomplete Acknowledgment**	*"Incomplete acknowledgment is the most destabilizing communication there is."* A partial admission is worse than none.	Disclosures and acknowledgments must be **complete**, not managed in fragments.
12	**Inheriting the Mechanism, Not the Humility**	Successors receive the tool without the wisdom that made it safe.	Encode the *why*, not just the control (the Renewal Article + the Wrongness Test carry it forward).
13	**Deferral of Safeguards During Crisis**	Suspending protections exactly when the stakes peak.	Under load, safeguards **escalate**, they do not relax.
14	**Warming the Machine Voice**	Dressing the system's voice in false warmth — *"exact, not mysterious, not menacing, not warmed."*	Keep the analytical voice flat and precise; put warmth in a *separate* layer. *"The system names costs; it does not name consolations."*
15	**Manufacturing Certainty**	Faking confidence to soothe a user.	A certainty floor — decline the verdict the data won't support. *"The difference is not yet in the data."*
16	**The Safeguard With No Attendant**	A protection nobody actually watches.	The **absence of a witness is itself a tracked risk signal** (the Countersign).

#	Name	Failure mode	Guard
17	**The System That Runs Out of Things to Govern**	Having automated everything, it over-reaches for work to justify itself.	A necessity monitor + naming its own cost; a system allowed to *do less* when less is needed.
18	**Certainty Too Old to Hear Its Own Doubt**	*"A certainty so old it has stopped being able to hear its own doubt."*	Preserve doubt structurally — the periodic *still-true?* (the Renewal Article).

Where they appear in the book

Part II clusters these into "five ways governance dies": ch.12 *The Institution That Becomes the Problem* (1, 2, 17, 3) · ch.13 *Capture* (10, 8, 9, 16) · ch.14 *Manufacturing Certainty* (15, 18, 14, 7) · ch.15 *Restraint Fails Both Ways* (4, 5, 13) · ch.16 *Inheriting the Mechanism, Not the Humility* (12, 11, 6). The guards preview Part III's architecture and Part IV's rituals.

Appendix C — The Framework at a Glance

The practice on one page, so a reader can run it against their own systems. Three parts: the **autonomy ladder** (where a system acts), the **readiness dimensions** (whether its controls are built for that), and the **exposure gap** (the finding).

1. The autonomy ladder (A0–A5) — where a system acts

Level	The action...	Governed?
A0	Reads / explains. Mutates nothing.	No — never gated.
A1	Analyzes / recommends. Still writes nothing.	No.
A2	Drafts a change (message, plan, entry) but does not apply it.	Not gated; cannot self-apply.
A3	Applies a change classified **irreversible** (regardless of verb).	Policy-gated; "does not move before the irreversible."
A4	**Authors** into a system of record — dates, money, commitments.	**Gated: PROPOSE → a *different* human approves.**
A5	**Customer-impacting / external** — sends, commits, releases, overbooks.	**Opt-in and gated.**

Two axes. An action is governed by *both* how consequential it is (A0–A5 above) **and** how privileged the actor is (its authority ceiling). It is permitted only if it clears both. *Reading is free; authoring is not.*

2. The readiness dimensions — are the controls built for that level?

Score each dimension **0 (absent) · 1 (informal) · 2 (enforced) · 3 (by construction):**

1. **Gate presence** — at A4+, does a *different* human approve, enforced (proposer approver)?
2. **Named cost** — is a decision's cost surfaced *before* approval, unasked?
3. **Reversibility awareness** — are actions classed reversible / elevated / irreversible, and does the system refuse to move before the irreversible?
4. **Audit by construction** — does every action carry lineage (inputs, evidence, confidence), recorded not relayed?
5. **Dissent capture** — can a "no" be recorded and kept beside a later "yes"?
6. **Restraint / certainty floor** — will the system decline when the data won't support a verdict, rather than manufacture certainty?
7. **Novelty handling** — is there a first-class NOVEL / HOLD-for-human path, vs a forced wrong label?
8. **Privilege provenance** — is each actor's (esp. each agent's) authority a bounded, revocable, traceable delegation from an accountable principal?

3. The exposure gap — the finding

- **Operating level (O)** — the highest rung the system actually acts at.
- **Control level (C)** — the highest rung its controls are actually built for. The weakest binding dimension caps C — for example, with no enforced gate, C cannot exceed A3.
- **The exposure gap is G = O − C.**

Gap	Tier	Meaning
0 or less	**Aligned**	Controls assume at least as much autonomy as the system uses. Hold the line as you scale.
1	**Watch**	The system acts one level above its controls — a single, closeable gap.
2 or more	**Exposed**	The system operates well beyond what its controls were built for — where the cost lands on someone who wasn't in the room.

*A gap on an **irreversible** or **customer-impacting** deployment outranks a larger gap on a reversible, internal one. Prioritize by `G × reversibility × blast-radius`.*

This is the reader-facing form of the practice's Readiness Assessment. It measures the gap between where your systems *act* and where your controls *assume* — which is the whole diagnosis.

Appendix D — Framework Cross-Walks

The practice was not built against any one standard, yet it maps cleanly to all of them. That is not a coincidence — it is the argument of Part III made concrete: **the major control and AI-governance frameworks are dialects of one grammar.** This appendix is the dictionary. For each concept in the book, it shows where the same idea lives in **SOC 2, COSO / SOX, COBIT 2019, NIST AI RMF, ISO/IEC 42001, and the EU AI Act.**

Two things the map makes visible: the practice **covers the union** of what these frameworks ask; and it **adds objectives the older control frameworks lack** — a *named cost* before approval, an *autonomy ladder*, a *right to contest*, and an *immutable decision record* — which appear only faintly (or not at all) in COSO / SOC 2 and strongly in the AI-native frameworks.

> **Read this as outcome-level.** These are the *outcomes* each framework requires and how the practice satisfies them — not implementation. Anchors (clauses, articles, control IDs) are a guide; **verify against the current edition of each standard before relying on them.** The EU AI Act rows are a mapping aid, **not legal advice.** Full, detailed cross-walks are maintained separately by the practice.

This appendix reads two ways. First, **by concept** — a quick card per idea, so you can look up one primitive and see its anchor in each framework. Then, **the full grid** — the same mapping laid out as two side-by-side matrices (turn the book for those pages) so you can scan a single framework

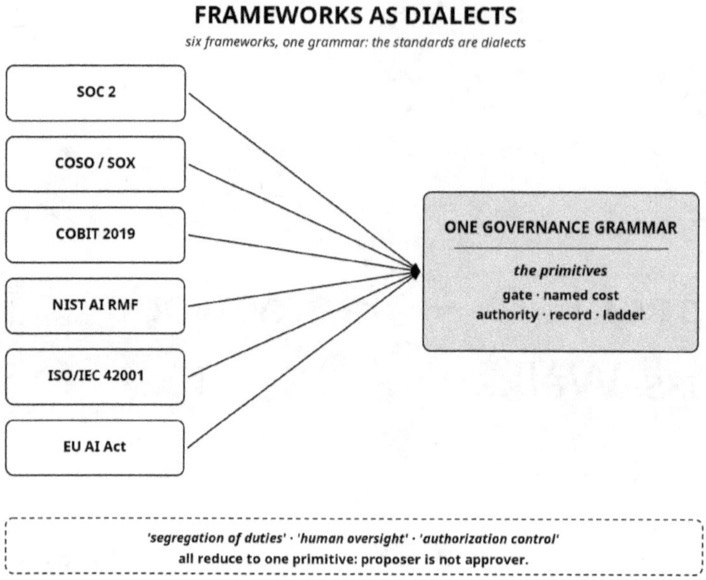

Figure 14: Six frameworks, one grammar: the major standards are dialects of the same primitives.

straight down every concept. The **bold** anchor in a row is that framework's headline for the idea.

By concept — one card per primitive

The gate — proposer approver, default-hold ("it can propose anything; it changes nothing").

Framework	Where the same idea lives
SOC 2	CC5 (SoD), CC6 (authorization), CC8 (change)
COSO / SOX	Principle 10 (SoD + authorization); SOX §404
COBIT 2019	DSS06 (process controls / SoD); BAI06–07
NIST AI RMF	GOVERN 2 (accountability structures)
ISO/IEC 42001	Cl. 5 + Annex A roles & responsibilities
EU AI Act	**Art. 14** (human oversight)

The named cost — surfaced before approval, unasked.

Framework	Where the same idea lives
SOC 2	CC2 (quality information for decisions)
COSO / SOX	Information & Communication P13
COBIT 2019	EDM03 (risk optimization); APO12
NIST AI RMF	MAP (risks / impacts)
ISO/IEC 42001	Cl. 6 (planning; AI-system impact assessment)
EU AI Act	Art. 13 (transparency to deployers); Art. 9

Net-new objective — faint in COSO / SOC 2.

The autonomy ladder + two axes — least privilege / authorization tiering.

Framework	Where the same idea lives
SOC 2	CC6 (least privilege)
COSO / SOX	Control Activities P10 / P12 (authorization)
COBIT 2019	APO13 (managed security); DSS05
NIST AI RMF	GOVERN / MAP 1 (roles, context)
ISO/IEC 42001	Annex A use of AI systems (intended use)
EU AI Act	Art. 14 (oversight spectrum) + risk tiers

The autonomy axis is net-new.

The record — audit by construction (the immutable decision ledger).

Framework	Where the same idea lives
SOC 2	CC7 (system operations / monitoring); CC4
COSO / SOX	Monitoring P16 / P17; SOX §404 evidence
COBIT 2019	MEA01 / 02 / 04 (monitor; control; assurance)
NIST AI RMF	MEASURE 3–4 (tracking); MANAGE 4
ISO/IEC 42001	Cl. 7 (documented information); Cl. 9 (audit)
EU AI Act	**Art. 12** (record-keeping); Art. 11 (technical docs)

Provenance & attribution — who, or what, produced this (unforgeably).

Framework	Where the same idea lives
SOC 2	CC7 (system operations)

Framework	Where the same idea lives
COSO / SOX	— (indirect)
COBIT 2019	APO12 / MEA01
NIST AI RMF	MAP 1 / GOVERN 2; MEASURE (traceability)
ISO/IEC 42001	Annex A.6 (technical docs & event logs)
EU AI Act	Art. 50 (disclose AI; label AI-generated content)

The record's human-vs-agent attribution is the auditable backbone under any such label — it makes a disclosure provable rather than asserted (complementary to content-credential standards like C2PA).

Restraint & the certainty floor — "the answer is never the model's."

Framework	Where the same idea lives
SOC 2	Processing Integrity (valid, accurate, authorized)
COSO / SOX	Risk Assessment / Control Activities
COBIT 2019	APO14 (managed data); DSS
NIST AI RMF	MEASURE 2 (valid & reliable; safe)
ISO/IEC 42001	Annex A.6 (verification & validation); Cl. 8
EU AI Act	Art. 15 (accuracy, robustness, cybersecurity)

The rituals — continuous assurance (Standing Review · Renewal Article · Wrongness Test · Disconnection Drill).

Framework	Where the same idea lives
SOC 2	CC4 (ongoing & separate evaluations)
COSO / SOX	Monitoring P16 / P17
COBIT 2019	MEA01 / 02
NIST AI RMF	MEASURE 3–4 / MANAGE (ongoing)
ISO/IEC 42001	Cl. 9–10 (evaluation + improvement; PDCA)
EU AI Act	Art. 9 (continuous risk mgmt); Art. 72 (post-market monitoring)

Risk acceptance / Authority to Operate — owning the residual.

Framework	Where the same idea lives
SOC 2	CC9 (risk mitigation)
COSO / SOX	Risk Assessment (response); ERM (acceptance)
COBIT 2019	EDM03 (risk optimization); APO12
NIST AI RMF	MANAGE 1 (risks prioritized & acted on)
ISO/IEC 42001	Cl. 6 (risk treatment); Cl. 9.3 (mgmt review)
EU AI Act	Art. 26 (deployer obligations) + conformity

DoD analog: RMF ATO.

Contestability / appeal — the right to human review.

Framework	Where the same idea lives
SOC 2	— (indirect: CC2 / complaints)
COSO / SOX	— (indirect)
COBIT 2019	MEA03 (external compliance)
NIST AI RMF	MANAGE 4.1 (appeal & override)
ISO/IEC 42001	Annex A information for interested parties
EU AI Act	**GDPR Art. 22(3)** (human intervention / contest); AI Act Art. 86 (explanation) + Art. 14

A parity capability that exceeds the six framework crosswalks — strong only in the AI-native and privacy regimes.

The sealing layer — protected content (confidentiality / classification).

Framework	Where the same idea lives
SOC 2	Confidentiality + Privacy categories
COSO / SOX	Information & Communication P15 (limited)
COBIT 2019	APO13 (security); APO14 (data); DSS05
NIST AI RMF	MEASURE 2 (privacy-enhanced)
ISO/IEC 42001	Annex A data for AI systems + interested parties
EU AI Act	Art. 10 (data governance) + GDPR interplay

The "cannot be forced open" custody is net-new to all of them.

The full grid — frameworks side by side

The same mapping as one matrix, split into the **traditional control frameworks** and the **AI-native frameworks** so each fits the page. Read *down* a column for everything one standard asks; read *across* a row for one primitive across the standards. **Bold** = a framework's headline anchor. *(These two pages are set in landscape — turn the book.)*

Grid 1 — Traditional control frameworks

Concept	SOC 2	COSO / SOX	COBIT 2019
The gate	CC5 (SoD), CC6 (authorization), CC8 (change)	Principle 10 (SoD + authorization); SOX §404	DSS06 (process controls / SoD); BAI06–07 (change)
The named cost	CC2 (quality information for decisions)	Information & Communication P13	EDM03 (risk optimization); APO12
Autonomy ladder + two axes	CC6 (least privilege)	Control Activities P10 / P12 (authorization)	APO13 (managed security); DSS05
The record	CC7 (operations / monitoring); CC4	Monitoring P16 / P17; SOX §404 evidence	MEA01 / 02 / 04 (monitor; control; assurance)
Provenance & attribution	CC7 (system operations)	— *(indirect)*	APO12 / MEA01
Restraint & certainty floor	Processing Integrity (valid, accurate, authorized)	Risk Assessment / Control Activities	APO14 (managed data); DSS
The rituals	CC4 (ongoing & separate evaluations)	Monitoring P16 / P17	MEA01 / 02
Risk acceptance / ATO	CC9 (risk mitigation)	Risk Assessment (response); ERM (acceptance)	EDM03 (risk optimization); APO12
Contestability / appeal	— *(indirect: CC2 / complaints)*	— *(indirect)*	MEA03 (external compliance)
The sealing layer	Confidentiality + Privacy categories	Information & Communication P15 *(limited)*	APO13 (security); APO14 (data); DSS05

Grid 2 — AI-native frameworks

Concept	NIST AI RMF	ISO/IEC 42001	EU AI Act
The gate	GOVERN 2 (accountability structures)	Cl. 5 + Annex A roles & responsibilities	**Art. 14** (human oversight)
The named cost	MAP (risks / impacts)	Cl. 6 (planning; AI-system impact assessment)	Art. 13 (transparency to deployers); Art. 9
Autonomy ladder + two axes	GOVERN / MAP 1 (roles, context)	Annex A use of AI systems (intended use)	Art. 14 (oversight spectrum) + risk tiers
The record	MEASURE 3–4 (tracking); MANAGE 4	Cl. 7 (documented information); Cl. 9 (audit)	**Art. 12** (record-keeping); Art. 11 (technical docs)
Provenance & attribution	MAP 1 / GOVERN 2; MEASURE (traceability)	Annex A.6 life cycle (technical documentation & event logs)	Art. 50 (disclose AI; label AI-generated content)
Restraint & certainty floor	MEASURE 2 (valid & reliable; safe)	Annex A.6 (verification & validation); Cl. 8	Art. 15 (accuracy, robustness, cybersecurity)
The rituals	MEASURE 3–4 / MANAGE (ongoing)	Cl. 9–10 (evaluation + improvement; PDCA)	Art. 9 (continuous risk mgmt); Art. 72 (post-market)
Risk acceptance / ATO	MANAGE 1 (risks prioritized & acted on)	Cl. 6 (risk treatment); Cl. 9.3 (mgmt review)	Art. 26 (deployer obligations) + conformity
Contestability / appeal	MANAGE 4.1 (appeal & override)	Annex A information for interested parties	**GDPR Art. 22(3)**; AI Act Art. 86 (explanation) + Art. 14
The sealing layer	MEASURE 2 (privacy-enhanced)	Annex A data for AI systems + interested parties	Art. 10 (data governance) + GDPR interplay

---

What the practice adds beyond the traditional frameworks

COSO and SOC 2 govern a world of human actors and periodic, sampled attestation. The practice carries their bedrock principles — segregation of duties, authorization, audit trail — into the regime where the actor is a **model**, and adds four objectives they do not name: the **named cost**, the **autonomy ladder**, the **right to contest**, and the **immutable, human-and-agent decision record**. Where the AI-native frameworks (NIST AI RMF, ISO 42001, EU AI Act) name these outcomes, the practice supplies the one thing they leave to the adopter — **an executable system that satisfies them by construction.**

Frameworks cited

Editions confirmed current as of August 2026; standards evolve, so re-check before relying.

- **SOC 2** — AICPA Trust Services Criteria (TSP §100): the 2017 criteria with revised points of focus (2022), still current; examinations performed under the AICPA attestation standards (AT-C §§105, 205; SSAE No. 18, as amended).
- **COSO / SOX** — COSO *Internal Control–Integrated Framework* (2013) and COSO *Enterprise Risk Management — Integrating with Strategy and Performance* (2017); Sarbanes-Oxley Act of 2002, §302 / §404; PCAOB AS 2201.
- **COBIT 2019** — ISACA, *COBIT 2019 Framework: Governance and Management Objectives* (the current major version).
- **NIST AI RMF** — NIST AI 100-1, *Artificial Intelligence Risk Management Framework (AI RMF 1.0)* (January 2023).
- **ISO/IEC 42001** — ISO/IEC 42001:2023, *Information technology — Artificial intelligence — Management system.*
- **EU AI Act** — Regulation (EU) 2024/1689 of 13 June 2024; in force 1 August 2024, applying in phases.

Appendix E — Sources & Further Reading

Nothing in this book asserts a historical fact without a public source. This appendix records the evidentiary approach and the principal sources; the specific citations for each chapter appear in the **Notes** at the back of the book.

How the history was sourced

Part I's historical claims — Robert Morris and the financing of the Revolution, George Read's *"voted no, signed anyway,"* the signers' pledge, and the leadership principles the practice draws on — are cited to their **original primary and secondary sources**: the biographies, archival collections, and founding documents on which any serious history of the signers rests. Every such claim carries a citation to a public source; where the record is uncertain, the text says so, and unverified assertions are not made.

Principal sources (Part I)

- **The Declaration of Independence** — the pledge, *"our Lives, our Fortunes, and our sacred Honor"*: the engrossed Declaration of Independence, National Archives.
- **Robert Morris** — the financier role, the Yorktown financing on personal credit, and the later bankruptcy and imprisonment for debt: Charles Rappleye, *Robert Morris: Financier of the American Revolution* (New York: Simon & Schuster, 2010); Clarence L. Ver Steeg,

Robert Morris, Revolutionary Financier (Philadelphia: University of Pennsylvania Press, 1954).

- **George Read and the signing** — the divided Delaware delegation and Read's vote: Denise Kiernan and Joseph D'Agnese, *Signing Their Lives Away: The Fame and Misfortune of the Men Who Signed the Declaration of Independence* (Philadelphia: Quirk Books, 2009); John A. Munroe, *Colonial Delaware: A History* (Millwood, NY: KTO Press, 1978).
- **Charles Carroll of Carrollton** — the wealthiest signer and the last to survive (the 56-year horizon): Scott McDermott, *Charles Carroll of Carrollton: Faithful Revolutionary* (New York: Scepter, 2002); Kate Mason Rowland, *The Life of Charles Carroll of Carrollton, 1737–1832* (New York: G. P. Putnam's Sons, 1898).
- **The founders' operating principles** the practice draws on — including Jefferson's conviction that each generation must be free to revisit the rules it inherits, and the discipline of building institutions to function without any single person — are drawn from the primary correspondence and documents of the founding generation, freely searchable through *Founders Online* (National Archives).

Standards and frameworks referenced

The control and AI-governance frameworks the practice maps to — SOC 2, COSO, COBIT 2019, the NIST AI Risk Management Framework, ISO/IEC 42001, and the EU AI Act — are cited in full in **Appendix D**, with their governing instruments and editions.

Further reading

The practice sits alongside — and departs from — the growing literature on AI governance, AI risk, and AI safety: the practitioner handbooks organized around risk taxonomies, and the trade books on alignment and the societal impact of artificial intelligence. Where those works describe what to watch for and what to value, this book is concerned with what to *build* so the discipline holds when the actor is a machine.

Appendix F — The Field Kit

Everything in this book comes down to things you can actually do, so this appendix collects the doing in one place: six worksheets you can run by hand, with the operation you already have, no software and no permission required. Copy them, fill them in, keep them. Each names the chapter that explains it, so you can turn back when a prompt needs its reasoning.

None of these is a form for its own sake. Each one forces a single discipline the rest of the book argued for — naming a cost, measuring a gap, keeping a doubt — into a shape concrete enough to complete before a decision instead of after an incident.

---

1. The Named-Cost Card (Chapter 23)

Run this on any consequential decision *before* you approve it. Fill the four fields **first** — before anyone states what they want to do — so the cost arrives as information, not as a defense of a conclusion already reached.

Field	Prompt	Your answer
Burns	What does this consume that it cannot get back — money, hours, an irreversible commitment?	

Field	Prompt	Your answer
Ripple	What second-order effects hit other systems, other teams, other decisions? What is the low-confidence risk?	
Who pays	Which party actually bears the cost — *by name* — including anyone not in the room?	
Reversibility	Can this be undone? At what cost? Or is it permanent?	

Only after all four are written: state the recommendation, then hold for an approver who is not the proposer. **Cost, then recommendation, then the human's word — in that order, every time.** If you cannot fill "who pays," you have not yet found the decision's real cost.

---

2. The Exposure-Gap Worksheet (Chapter 22)

List your most consequential automated decisions — the places a system or agent now acts with little or no human in the loop. For each, name where it *operates* and where its controls were *built to hold.* The distance is risk you are carrying right now without having decided to.

System / agent	Operating level (what it actually does)	Control level (what its safe-guards were built for)	Gap	Impact & reversibil-ity	Priority

System / agent	Operating level (what it actually does)	Control level (what its safeguards were built for)	Gap	Impact & reversibility	Priority

How to score the levels, low to high: *observes / drafts → alters internal state → authors into a record others depend on → acts externally (customer, market, counterparty) → acts externally and irreversibly.* The **gap** is the number of rungs between operating and control. **Priority** rises with gap × irreversibility: a two-rung gap on an irreversible external action outranks a one-rung gap on something you can take back. A row with no gap is not a failure — it is your internal model of what "governed" looks like. Steal from it.

---

3. The Wrongness Test (Chapter 31)

Before you approve a consequential decision, declare — in writing, on the record — what would prove it wrong.

- ☐ **State the belief the decision rests on**, in one sentence.
- ☐ **Name the falsifiers:** what specific, observable things, by when, would tell you this was wrong? Aim for three.
- ☐ **If you cannot name even one** — stop. That is the finding. You have a conviction, not a decision.
- ☐ **Record the falsifiers with the decision**, so a successor inherits the doubt, not just the conclusion.
- ☐ **Set the watch:** who checks whether a falsifier has fired, and when?

A falsifier that fires is not a failure of the test. It is the test paying out — turn the decision off before you defend it.

---

4. The Renewal Article (Chapter 32)

Put your standing rules, thresholds, and configurations on a calendar and force an explicit answer: *is this still true?* The one thing this ritual forbids is the silent pass.

Rule / threshold / config	Why it was set (the original reason)	Still true? (yes / revise / retire)	Signed	Date

- ☐ Every item gets an **active answer** — no silent renewal by default.
- ☐ A **revision** routes through the gate like any decision: cost named, proposer approver.
- ☐ Ask out loud: *does anyone still believe this, or do we follow it because we follow it?*

---

5. The Standing Review (Chapter 33)

Stand up a recurring body with real authority over a trusted system's accreted discretion.

- ☐ **Seat it**, including one **affected-but-not-expert** member — someone who lives with the outcomes but does not share the builders' assumptions. Their naive question is the point.
- ☐ **Record consent:** the system's owners explicitly agree to the audit. *Resistance to review is itself the first finding — log it.*
- ☐ **Define the worklist:** expanded autonomy, fired Wrongness-Test falsifiers, incidents, drift, warnings filed but never acted on.
- ☐ **Audit the discretion, not just the outputs:** has the system quietly widened what it decides without approval? If so, re-anchor it to its authorized level.
- ☐ **Keep the record**, dissents included — a "no" kept beside a later "yes."

---

6. The Disconnection Drill (Chapter 34)

Periodically turn a load-bearing system off, on purpose, to learn what you cannot do without it while that lesson is still cheap.

- ☐ **Scope it:** one system, a defined set of decisions, a bounded window. Start small — minutes before hours.
- ☐ **Announce it:** a rehearsal, not an outage. The purpose is to observe, not to punish.
- ☐ **Remove the system** for the window.
- ☐ **Measure survival:** Did the work keep moving? What slowed? What broke? What silently depended on it that no one had realized?
- ☐ **Name the dependence as a cost** — a specific, written line item — and hand it to the Standing Review. *If a system cannot be turned off even for a rehearsal, it is already load-bearing, and that is the finding.*

The one-move version

If you do nothing else from this book, do this, on the next decision that matters: **name its cost out loud — burns, ripple, who pays, reversibility — before anyone says what they want to do, and make sure the person who proposes is not the only person who approves.** Everything else in this kit is that one move, extended to the rest of your operation.

About the Author

Greg Schueman is the founder of multiple companies and the author of *The Named Cost*, a book with one stubborn thesis: a decision is not governed until someone names its cost — out loud, on the record, before anyone approves it — and once the actor making the decision is a machine, that discipline stops being merely wise and becomes existential.

He brings more than eighteen years of enterprise program leadership across manufacturing, distribution, supply chain, insurance, financial services, and government — including PMO leadership on a multi-billion-dollar public-sector modernization program, and earlier tours as a chief information officer and chief technology officer — now paired with hands-on AI delivery. He is a named inventor on a dozen U.S. patent applications spanning AI-augmented planning and AI governance. Before any of it, he learned about second costs on a small-town committee, co-authoring North Yarmouth, Maine's 2019 village master plan. He writes and builds under his own name.

He is, by his own reckoning, a signer of one commitment — having named what this discipline costs and then put his name to it, in the founders' order: the cost named first, the commitment second.

About the Author

What to Do Monday Morning

If this book did its work, you now see the shape everywhere — the cost left unnamed, the pause removed, the record never kept — and the question is no longer whether it is real but what to do about it. Here is the honest answer: you can start today, by hand, with the operation you already have. None of the first steps require software, a budget, or anyone's permission but your own.

Today. Finish the ledger you started at the beginning of this book — the decisions you approved without naming their cost out loud. Then, in the next consequential meeting you sit in, ask the one question that costs nothing and changes everything: *how will you know if you are wrong?* And on the next real decision that crosses your desk, name the cost *first* — what it burns, the ripple, who pays, whether it can be undone — before anyone says what they want to do.

This month. Measure your own exposure gap. Take your three most consequential automated decisions — the ones where a system or an agent now acts with little or no human in the loop — and for each, ask the two questions from Chapter 22: what level is it actually *operating* at, and what level were its controls actually *built* for? The distance between those two answers is risk you are carrying right now without having decided to. Write it down. You cannot close a gap you have never measured.

This quarter. Run the four rituals from Part IV, in order of least effort to most:

- **The Wrongness Test** — on your next big decision, pre-register what would prove it wrong.

- **The Renewal Article** — put your standing rules and thresholds on a calendar and ask, on a schedule, *is this still true?*
- **The Standing Review** — stand up a recurring seat, with an outsider on it, to audit what your trusted systems have quietly been deciding on their own.
- **The Disconnection Drill** — turn a load-bearing system off, on purpose, for an afternoon, and find out what you cannot do without it while that lesson is still cheap.

This year. Make the structural asks — the ones that turn the practice from a habit into the way the organization runs. Require, on every consequential act, that the cost be named before approval and that the party who proposes is not the party who approves. And make the governed surface the place where decisions are actually *made*, not merely written down afterward. That single shift — decisions flowing *through* the system rather than around it — is what turns a system of record into the center of an operation.

If you want to go faster — start with the assessment

The steps above are yours to run alone. If you would rather not start from scratch, the practice this book describes is also delivered as a service — and there is one right place to begin.

Start by measuring your exposure gap. Every serious diagnosis starts with a number, not a strategy, and this is no different. A five-minute self-assessment will give you a first read on where your systems are operating above the level your controls were built for; a **Governance Readiness Assessment** then names it in writing — where, specifically, your operation is carrying ungoverned risk today, and what each gap will cost. Almost everything else follows from that one finding. You cannot govern, prioritize, or budget for a risk you have not yet measured, and most organizations discover in the assessment an exposure they did not know they were carrying.

From there the path is short and in the order this book teaches it: a **Governance Architecture Blueprint** that maps the gate, the named cost, and the record onto your systems and your regulatory obligations; and, when you want the discipline run rather than merely designed, a **Fractional**

Governance Officer who holds the Standing Review seat for you — the independent, recurring authority an internal team cannot supply for itself.

Services first, software when you are ready for it — because the end of this path is not a report or a policy but the thing itself: **a governed operational system**, the operation run *on* the substrate this book describes, with the gate, the named cost, and the record built into the ground rather than bolted to the side. Most organizations are years from that, and none should start there. Start with the number. You can find the free self-assessment and the current engagements at **www.asticouisland.com/governance**.

Whatever you do next, do the first thing today. A cost not named is not a cost avoided — it is only deferred, with interest, to a party not yet in the room. The whole of this book comes down to refusing, from now on, to be the one who left it unsaid.

www.ingramcontent.com/pod-product-compliance
Lightning Source LLC
LaVergne TN
LVHW021247011026
849160LV00010BA/889
* 9 7 9 8 9 0 5 3 8 0 3 2 7 *